GOOD to the GRAIN

Baking with Whole-Grain Flours

KIM BOYCE

with **Amy Scattergood**

Photographs by **QUENTIN BACON**

stewart, tabori & chang | new york

Published in 2010 by Stewart, Tabori & Chang
An imprint of ABRAMS

Text copyright © 2010 Kim Boyce
Photographs copyright © 2010 Quentin Bacon

Library of Congress Cataloging-in-Publication Data
Boyce, Kim.
    Good to the grain : baking with whole-grain flours /
by Kim Boyce with Amy Scattergood.10
        p. cm.
    Includes index.
    ISBN 978-1-58479-830-9
1. Cookery (Cereals) 2. Baking. 3. Grain. I. Scattergood, Amy,
1964-
II. Title.
    TX808.B596 2010
    641.6'31—dc22   2009034381

Editor: Luisa Weiss
Designer: Susi Oberhelman
Production Manager: Tina Cameron

The text of this book was composed in Sentinel and Gotham

Printed and bound in China
10 9 8 7 6 5 4 3 2 1

Stewart, Tabori & Chang books are available at special discounts when purchased in quantity for premiums and promotions as well as fundraising or educational use. Special editions can also be created to specification. For details, contact specialsales@abramsbooks.com or the address below.

THE ART OF BOOKS SINCE 1949

115 West 18th Street
New York, NY 10011
www.abramsbooks.com

Contents

Foreword

Since there are so many cookbooks on the shelves these days, I feel very strongly that if you are going to write one, it should be something nobody has done before, and with *Good to the Grain*, Kim Boyce has clearly met that standard. Before I'd eaten a bite from any of the recipes, I looked at the table of contents and thought, "Wow! This isn't just another collection of recycled recipes. These are truly original." When I actually tasted the baked goods that came from these recipes, I was convinced Kim had created a book that really had a reason to be on the shelves, a book that people would discover was invaluable, and one they would come to love.

When Kim first told me about her idea for a baking book that utilized whole-grain in place of refined white flour, I knew that if anyone could pull it off, she could. I've known Kim since she came to work for me as the pastry chef at Campanile in 2000, and I had total confidence in her from the very beginning. I had always worked closely with my pastry chefs at Campanile, but at the time I hired Kim, I was ready to start giving up some of the day-to-day responsibilities of that job, and Kim turned out to be the perfect person to take over. She possessed all the qualities I admire in a baker—the same ones I have always aspired to myself: Her presentations were fairly simple, her desserts tasted as good as they looked (and looked as good as they tasted!), and she was willing to do whatever it took to develop a recipe to a point where it was absolutely as good as it could be, no matter how long and painstaking the process. Naturally, the same qualities that made her an exceptional employee come through in this exceptional book.

My priority as both a baker and an eater is not health but flavor. What makes the recipes in this book so special is that—whether you care about whole grains or not—they are truly delicious. A perfect example is Kim's Chocolate Chip Cookie recipe. I am a big fan of chocolate chip cookies, and I have strong opinions about what makes a good one. I like the chocolate to be chopped by hand, and I like the cookies to have a nice crackle on top from having risen in the oven and then fallen when they cooled. This is the indication that a chocolate chip cookie will be chewy and moist (as opposed to cakey or dry), and Kim's cookie has that. The texture and flavor of the cookie

are in no way compromised by being made with whole-wheat flour, and the same holds true for every recipe I tried from this book.

Kim's Muscovado Sugar Cake has the deep, complex molasses flavor of the muscovado sugar without being too sweet—just the sort of thing you'd love to have with a cup of coffee or tea.

What makes the **recipes** in this book **so special** is that—whether **you care** about whole grains **or not**—they are **truly delicious**.

The fact that the cake is made with amaranth flour is almost incidental. Her Hazelnut Muffins have a light, airy crumb and are absolutely nothing like the leaden things you might expect from muffins made with whole-grain flour (in this case, teff flour). The same goes for her Sand Cookies, which are buttery, crumbly, and just *so* good. If she hadn't told me they were made with Kamut flour, it never would have occurred to me that there was anything whole-grain about them.

Whole grains aside, the recipes here reminded me of just how creative a baker Kim is. A perfect example is what she does with granola. Most people's variations on granola have to do with adding cashews, sunflower seeds, dried apricots, and the like. But Kim has made a granola using oats and seeds (no nuts), with a touch of cayenne added to the mix—I wouldn't have thought to do that in a million years, and yet it is utterly delicious.

What makes Kim an exceptional baker is that she does not stop short of perfection. In so many cases, pastry chefs will get the basic concept for a dish down; they get a recipe *almost* there—and then they stop. Kim, on the other hand, knows the difference between almost-there and extraordinary—something I'm not sure can be taught. There is no doubt in my mind that as light and tender as her Beaten Biscuits are, or as moist and delicious as the Coconut Cookies taste, these were not her first attempts, but rather the results of endless tinkering.

In addition to her relentless pursuit of perfection, Kim has the technical skill necessary to achieve this level of quality. A whole-grain baguette, for instance, might have the heft and texture of something you'd be more tempted to use as a weapon than to eat. But Kim's expertise has produced a baguette with a crispness to the crust and a lightness to the interior that I don't normally associate with whole-grain breads. When I tasted it, I was certain it was exactly the baguette that Kim had set out to make. Had I ever set out to achieve a whole-grain baguette, it was also the one *I* would have wanted to make.

My first impulse when I'm tasting a dish or a baked good I've never had before is to think about how I would do it differently, how I would improve upon it. I love it when I come across something and think, "This is perfect! I wouldn't change a thing." Time after time as I ate my way through *Good to the Grain*, I thought, "That's exactly how I would have done it." That's the sweetness I would have wanted in that scone, and the texture I would have wanted for that cookie. That's the size I would have cut the biscuit, and the way I would have finished the Danish. For whatever it's worth, Kim Boyce's recipes in *Good to the Grain* are my idea of perfection.

—NANCY SILVERTON

What makes Kim an **exceptional baker** is that she **does not stop** short of **perfection**. Kim knows the difference between **almost-there** and **extraordinary**—something I'm not sure can be taught.

Introduction

I trained as a pastry chef, first apprenticing with Sherry Yard at the original Spago in West Hollywood and later working closely with Nancy Silverton at Campanile in Los Angeles. It didn't seem to me that baking could get much better than that. But when I left the professional kitchen to start a family, to my amazement, it did.

My kitchen was being remodeled and I had taken to strolling the grocery aisles, searching for ways to make meals quickly and with few ingredients. On one such outing, I found a bag of Bob's Red Mill 10 Grain Pancake Mix and brought it home. Later that day, my young daughter, Lola, was on my hip and hungry. To get dinner on the table quickly, I grabbed the pancake mix, along with some of my daughter's homemade puréed beets and apples, milk, eggs, and butter from the refrigerator. I whipped up a batch of pancakes—I was literally cooking on my dining room table with an electric griddle—and within minutes, they were on the griddle, puffing ever so slightly and turning a warm burgundy hue. So simple, so ordinary, and so delicious! I started wondering about the flours that were in that mix, and that's when I had my epiphany: Cooking with whole-grain flours brought so much more flavor to the plate.

Who knew that after years of *financiers, sabayons,* and puff pastry, it would be a pancake that would change the way I baked? Inspired to know more about how whole-grain flours worked, I filled the glass jars in my kitchen with flours: whole-wheat and buckwheat, flours ground from spelt and corn and oats. I stood in the baking aisles of grocery and natural-food stores, looking at all the flours I had never heard of, much less used. Soon jars of amaranth, quinoa, and teff flours were lining my countertops, all these unusual grains adding new textures, colors, and tastes to my pastries.

I soon discovered that working with whole grains isn't simply a question of trading a bag of white flour for one filled with whole wheat—if it were that straightforward, my kitchen epiphany would have ended with the batch of pancakes that night, and you wouldn't be reading this book.

Baking with whole-grain flours is about balance, about figuring out how to get the right combination of structure and flavor from flours that don't act the same way as regular white

flour. Getting the texture right was a challenge. There is a reason whole-wheat pastry has a bad reputation. The muffins I mixed using exclusively whole-grain flour came out dense and tough, sometimes almost leaden. Pancakes were heavy and limp. The elegant lift and structure of pastries I'd made with white flours were nowhere to be found. I found myself getting discouraged as I learned to bake with these whole-grain flours and almost stopped using them altogether. Maybe *this* is the reason more people aren't baking with whole-grain flours, I thought.

Then my husband, Thomas, whom I'd met in my early days on the line at Spago, urged me to go back to the basics, to return to a favorite old recipe to remind myself that I could still bake. I took his advice and baked an old standby, a single-bowl recipe for cream biscuits that relied on all-purpose flour. After those weeks elbow-deep in speckled, mottled flours, I was surprised to see how glaringly white the biscuits looked and how little flavor they had.

I decided to keep on trying. First I developed a simple muffin recipe as my guide. Then I began experimenting with various ratios of flours and found that by combining two kinds of flours—by sifting a cup of all-purpose flour with an equal amount of barley flour or dark whole-grain rye—I could get the light structure of a great muffin as well as the complex flavor of the whole-grain flours I'd come to love.

I began adding **whole-grain flours** not only to **muffins** and **pancakes**, but to **cookies** and **cakes as well**. The **flavor** was **fantastic**.

I began adding whole-grain flours not only to muffins and pancakes, but to cookies and cakes as well. I tested out more intricate recipes like breads and yeasted pastries. The flavor was fantastic. There were hints of dry grass or toasted nuts, an earthy or milky flavor, or the surprisingly sweet taste of malt or even caramel. There were so many dimensions to the flavors, and so many new ways I could explore them in baking. I realized that I was thinking differently about the way

I baked. Instead of relying on traditional sugars and spice or fruit, I was now using flour to add greater flavor to my recipes.

When I began working with these whole-grain flours, I was a little intimidated. Many of the flours were unfamiliar, sometimes with strong and unusual flavors. Anytime I would get

As I **focused** on the **individual flavors** of the **various flours**, I began to **appreciate** what was **unique about them**. I **soon found** that I **enjoyed baking** with them.

frustrated with the flours, I would want to return to what I knew. But then I thought about my time at Campanile and Nancy's approach to cooking, her way of respecting the ingredients even if they were difficult to use or had flavors that were tricky to work with. As I focused on the individual flavors of the various flours, I began to appreciate what was unique about them. I soon found that I enjoyed baking with them. As the flours came into their own, so did I. As I worked my way through different bags of flour, learning how each one behaved in my recipes, I began to trust my instincts.

Nancy had changed how I looked at desserts, in large part because of how she worked with fruit. I folded those lessons into my whole-grain baking, using fruit, honey, molasses, and homemade jams to give my recipes sweetness with some character, rather than the nondescript sweetness of white sugar. But just as with flour, there needs to be a balance. Recipes rely on some sugar for loft and tenderness, but adding some honey or molasses for sweetness gives many pastries more dimension.

Here I was, a mom baking at home for my family and friends. Most days I was in the kitchen mixing up muffins, pancakes, or quick breads, and I realized that I couldn't continue using the endless handfuls of sugar and white flour I had used during my professional years. But I couldn't

stop baking! Now with my newfound interest in whole-grain flours, pairing them with seasonal fruits for incredible flavor, and making them with less sugar and butter than I used to, I realized that I didn't *have* to stop baking. Baking at home was limited only by how many ingredients I had on hand and how much I wanted to spend on them. So I learned to be flexible and use what was available, first in how I cooked and eventually in how I developed the recipes for this book.

I wanted this book to be inspirational but also very practical. That's why the chapters that follow are organized by type of flour. Many of the whole-grain flours called for here may be difficult to find in your local stores (there is a list of sources on page 200), and they can have a short shelf life unless they are stored properly (see "Flour" on page 32). This way, when you discover a bag of spelt flour at your grocery store or teff flour at an Ethiopian market, you can flip to the relevant chapter and figure out what to do with it. You can learn about the flavors of each flour and how it works with other ingredients, then choose from a handful of recipes that use it. If you like that flour, you can bake your way through the other recipes in that chapter and use up the whole bag.

The joyful discovery in writing this cookbook was that the flours and the recipes made from them weren't just substitutes for the "real thing." What started out as a way to feed my daughter nutritious pancakes and muffins turned into my style of baking. I didn't have to sacrifice all my years of professional training and experience to feed my family—those years were the foundation for my future. These are not the fancy recipes of my former life as a restaurant pastry chef. They are the recipes I cook at home for my friends and family. And you can, too. Once you are comfortable with the recipes, use them as your guide. Be creative. Experiment. Swap out the flour in one recipe for that in another—the differences are amazing, but each recipe will stand proudly and deliciously on its own.

—KIM BOYCE

Technique

Technique is a way of **balancing** the **chaos** of the everyday world with a little **kitchen precision**.

For the overwhelming majority of home cooks, baking isn't about tempering chocolate or pulling sugar or making fancy layer cakes. It's about stirring a simple batter in a single bowl, or making a quick bread on a weekend morning. This is not to say that home baking isn't about technique. In fact, technique is just as important at home as it is in a professional kitchen—perhaps even more so, to offset the distractions of noise, phone calls, hungry kids to feed, and whatever else home life throws your way. There are also many variables that affect baking, such as weather, altitude, temperature, and accident. Technique is about figuring out how butter acts on a hot day, or how much liquid a piece of ripe fruit will give up when you cook it in hot syrup, or how much flour a bread dough needs to have.

Don't let technique intimidate you. Technique is a way of balancing the chaos of the everyday world with a little kitchen precision. It's about learning which elements require strict attention (cold butter, a specific oven) and which ones you can make up as you go along (don't have one ingredient? use something else). Technique means determining how to measure flour correctly, and remembering that there's a difference between a liquid and a dry measurement. And you don't need professional experience or a culinary degree to accomplish these things— just a little guidance.

To that end, this book is about technique, sifted throughout the recipes rather than compartmentalized separately. I'll tell you what you're doing and why, because a recipe should be an inspiration, not just a mathematical formula. Cooking requires paying attention—to your ingredients, to your tools, and to what is happening on your stove. But it should also be a lot of fun—your hands are going to get dirty, flour will scatter all over, and your sink will accumulate a lot of messy dishes. So, instead of an exhaustive catalog of various techniques, I offer here a brief list of the issues I think are the most important. Think about how they relate to your kitchen, and use them as guideposts.

Judicious Use of Flour

Flour is the building block of bread—perhaps the most basic of all foods—and the cornerstone of so much in the kitchen. But as fundamental as it is, flour is also an enormous variable. Use the wrong flour and your muffins can come out dense, but add the right one—or the right blend—and you can create something remarkable. The kind and amount of flour used can make the difference between dough that is soft and pliant and a mass that is unworkable. So choose your flour thoughtfully. Feel it, smell it, taste it, look at it. Consider its source. Check to see how old it is or if it's rancid. Know that a humid day or a change in altitude will affect how it works. The more you get to know the contents of the sacks and bags and canisters of flours in your kitchen, the better you'll be able to use them.

Measuring

How you measure flour will make a huge difference in what happens with your recipe. To measure flour, scoop up the flour a few times to lighten it before finally filling a measuring cup; then level off the top with the flat side of a knife or other kitchen utensil. To measure brown sugar, pack it lightly; don't cram it into the measuring cup. Also, pay attention to the measuring cups in your kitchen. There is a difference between a liquid measuring cup (for dairy, honey, or molasses) and a dry measuring cup (for flour and sugar), so be sure to use the right one. A note on scales: They are the most accurate way to bake, as they yield precise measurements each time. However, since many people don't own scales, myself included, in this book you will find measurements using cups and spoons.

The Condition of Butter

Butter plays a crucial role in pastries and baked goods. If a recipe calls for softened, cold, or even frozen butter, there's a reason. It can mean the difference between a light and flaky pastry and one that is tough and heavy, so read butter instructions carefully. If you see directions for working butter until it's the size of grains of rice, peas, or nuts, pay attention, and move quickly. The size of the butter is key in determining how tender your pastry will be. If it's hot outside, freeze the butter before rubbing it down into smaller, flatter pieces. It'll give you more wiggle room and let you find joy in this simple method instead of being frustrated by it.

Time

You may not realize it, but time is an all-important element. Fruits need time to ripen, dough needs time to rise, and ingredients need time to caramelize in the pan or the oven. Baked goods have very specific cooking times, and ignoring or forgetting them can jeopardize their outcome. Resting time is as crucial to a recipe as baking time, as it can allow the gluten in a dough to relax, or the flavors and spices in a mixture to develop. Even if you have the best kitchen instincts, the telephone might ring just when you're about to rotate a tray of muffins or pull a cake out of the oven, so if you don't have a timer, get one.

Temperature

The heat of your oven and the strength of your burners determine the outcome of your cooking. Baking at the correct temperature can mean the difference between a dark, chewy cookie with crisp edges and a pale, dry one, so get your oven calibrated, buy an inexpensive oven thermometer, and always keep the oven door closed during baking. Recipes work differently if you're using a large burner instead of a small one—for instance, sugar caramelizes faster or slower. Know this and take it into consideration; patience can make the difference between a decent product and a fantastic one. Cold temperature also plays a big role, as many doughs benefit from chilling or freezing before they're baked. Cooling hot mixtures like jams and syrups is also important to stop the cooking process quickly.

Even baking

All the baked goods in this book require even cooking in the oven. To ensure this, recipe instructions will call for you to rotate pans or sheets in the oven halfway through the baking time. If you are using two pans or sheets on the upper and lower thirds of the oven, place the top pan on the bottom rack and the bottom pan on the top rack at this halfway point and rotate the pan 180 degrees for even front-to-back baking. If you are using a single sheet or pan on the middle rack, rotate the pan 180 degrees for even front-to-back baking.

Tools

Clean out your cupboards and pare down the kitchen. Even with two chefs in the house our kitchen is fairly simple, and that's just how I like it. Who wants to have a bunch of stuff clogging up cupboards and gathering dust on countertops? Keep your kitchen space free so that you can store essentials, have ample prepping and cooking areas, and enjoy gathering for snacks and conversation. Here is a list of the tools I find most helpful in a streamlined kitchen, ones that are well worth the space they occupy.

Hands

The most important tools? You already possess them: Your hands. They're always there and always ready. My hands let me know when dough is moist enough or if a muffin or cake is ready to come out of the oven. Mixing biscuits and scones is best done by hand. Only hands can tell when the butter is the right size and when the dough has been mixed enough.

Making something by hand is a beautiful experience. It's reminiscent of days when our grandmothers and great-grandmothers had only their hands to work with. The feel and smell of the dough when you knead and press it with your fingers is so basic, even soulful.

Sifter

Sifting dry ingredients is a simple step called for in most baking recipes—one you might ignore. But I can't emphasize enough how important sifting is for the success of a quick bread or muffin. Sifting evenly distributes the ingredients, lightens flour (especially heavier-grade, whole-grain flour), and breaks up any clumps. When sifting the ingredients in this book, you will often find that coarser bits of bran, germ, brown sugar, and kosher salt are left behind. Don't throw them out; they add flavor and texture. Rub anything that doesn't come through the sifter with your hands to break up any clumps, then dump the bits back over the sifted flour. The only recipes for which I don't sift the dry ingredients are bread doughs.

A favorite kitchen tool is my old-fashioned, granny-style sifter. It's metal, with a sturdy handle that turns a hoop against the mesh. It was a gift from long ago, found at a garage sale.

Standing Mixer

If I could have only one electrical appliance in my kitchen (well, other than the stove and the refrigerator), I'd choose my standing mixer. My mixer is an old five-quart-capacity KitchenAid mixer that my mother-in-law gave me as a wedding gift. I use it to cream butter for cookies, cakes, and muffins and, more and more these days, to knead bread dough. My favorite place in the kitchen is standing next to that mixer with my arm resting on top of it, watching whatever glorious transformation is happening in that bowl. It's worth every inch of space it takes up on my counter.

Plastic Dough Scraper

This curved rectangle of flexible white plastic could easily be overlooked in the kitchen store, but it's amazingly useful. I treat mine like an extension of my hand, using it to scrape every last bit of batter out of a bowl. Its thinness gives a cleaner scrape than a thicker rubber spatula, and it's especially useful for removing tacky bread dough from the kitchen counter. I also find these scrapers invaluable for rolling out biscuits or scones that are sticking to a surface. With a slight lift of the scraper and a quick dusting of flour, you can continue rolling. I keep quite a few of these in my drawer.

The next time you are in Paris, stop at E.Dehillerin, the store for cooking utensils. They sell the sturdiest scraper I've ever used: a pale yellow, unevenly shaped disk of plastic that is slightly less flexible than most plastic scrapers commonly available in the United States. This little scraper makes me happier than any fancy handbag or pair of shoes ever could.

Metal Bench Scraper

This is the metal version of the dough scraper above. It does double duty, as both a knife and a way of cleaning my counters of flour and dried bits after a day of baking. Slicing spirals of dough or cutting scones is easy with this tool, as is portioning out dough for baguettes or rolls.

I have an especially fond appreciation for mine because it was handmade by Jack Stumpf, a gentleman who went with us every week to the Santa Monica farmers' market to forage for produce for the Campanile kitchen.

Small Metal Offset Spatula

If you're not a pastry chef, you might pass right by one of these in a cooking store or kitchen drawer. But they're super handy and have many more uses than you'd think. I use mine to flip crêpes, to lift muffins out of tins and cookies off of trays, to smooth out the tops of cakes, and to frost cupcakes. They are also helpful when I need to flip over delicate fruit that is caramelizing in a pan. They're small and flexible, so they can get into corners and crevices. I also use mine to swipe the tops of cups of flour for an even measure.

Serrated Offset Knife

My favorite knife is seven-and-a-half inches long, with serrated grooves that grasp easily onto chocolate and the delicate skins of stone fruit. I find it's easier to slice butter with this knife than with a straight-edged chef's knife, as the butter doesn't stick to its sides. I've noticed that I now rely on this knife far more than I should, for chopping things like onions and other vegetables, for which I really should use a standard chef's knife.

Cast-Iron Pan

A well-seasoned cast-iron pan can take the place of three or four other pans in your kitchen and, properly taken care of, can last a lifetime. The thing to know about cast iron is that the more you use it, the better the season (or finish) on it will be. My husband, Thomas, and I always used to argue over the cast-iron pan in our kitchen. I was the one ruining his hard-earned seasons by cooking tomatoes in the pan or washing it with soap and water. I have learned never to use soap and water to clean the pan—this can dry out the surface and, if left wet, can leave it susceptible to rusting. Instead, Thomas taught me to wipe it clean with a kitchen towel, rub it with coarse salt if food is sticking, and keep it well oiled. A good, well-seasoned pan will cook up crepes and pancakes like a dream, and you won't need to use nearly as much butter or oil when griddling.

Also, if your pan smells more savory than sweet, put it over a high flame and leave it to smoke and burn for five minutes. The flavor will be neutralized, and the pan will be ready to use for delicate pancakes, crêpes, or fruit once it has cooled.

A rasp—a fine grater or microplane—is an incredibly useful tool, especially for baking. I use mine to zest citrus and grate whole nutmeg and chocolate, all things that need a finer grade of holes than most box graters have. It's also invaluable for grating fresh ginger, which has tough threads. Grating ginger and citrus zest over the work bowl captures any juice from the ginger or oil essence from the zest, adding more flavor to the finished recipe. You can get fancy microplanes at cooking supply shops, or simple, inexpensive ones at hardware stores. I use the long, thin, rectangular type with no handle.

Box graters are also very useful, as they have larger holes and the box shape makes it easy to set the grater in a bowl or on a plate while you grate, instead of having to balance a flat grater over the bowl. I use mine for apples and pears, cheeses, and butter. Grating frozen butter is a perfect way to get great, flaky pastry.

You wouldn't think you'd find a fish spatula high on my list of favorite tools, but I reach for mine as often as I reach for my oven mitts. A fish spatula is about six inches long and three inches wide (curved and wider at the end, tapered towards the handle); it is made of metal but is thinner and more flexible than other metal spatulas, making it easier to use. I use mine to flip pancakes. It's also great for sliding large cookies off their baking sheets. And if you turn it over you can clean your pans and sheets with it. It's particularly helpful for removing bits of melted and hardened chocolate.

High-quality baking sheets are very important to me. I prefer the commercial kind: heavy-bottomed, made from sturdy metal (*not* nonstick), and with rims—so that nuts and oats don't fall out when I'm toasting them, and so there's something to grab onto when you're pulling a hot pan out of the oven. I buy them at restaurant supply stores.

Rasp

Box Grater

Fish Spatula

Baking Sheets

I never use Silpats. They're expensive, and I don't like the crust they give. I think their only place is in tuile work, which I don't do at home. I love parchment paper, but it's pricy (and wasteful) if you use it a lot. And it's one more box in my drawer, so I only use it for a few recipes.

When I was at Spago, Sherry Yard taught me a great trick. We'd roll cookie dough up in parchment paper and then use the rim of the baking sheet to press against the rolls of dough. This made for tight, secure logs of dough that can be stored in the refrigerator or freezer. The rolls are handy when you want a cookie warm from the oven, without the mess—just slice off and bake as many as you want.

Muffin Pans

All the muffin recipes in this book call for the same size muffin pan—because that's what I have and I love it. My muffin pan is a big metal one that just fits into my oven, with 24 cups of one-third-cup capacity each (measured with sugar, not water). I fill the cups with mounds of batter so that the muffins bake up into glorious domes with nice crunchy edges.

I love this pan not because I can make 24 muffins at a time, but because it's perfect for making half that. When I was at Campanile, we'd alternate the cups, filling every second cup and leaving the others empty. This meant that there was enough room for the muffins to have rounded tops and crusty edges without crowding into each other. It's a simple trick that might not occur to you unless you worked in a professional kitchen. And it allowed the muffins to bake evenly. Of course, you may use whatever size muffin tins you want—little ones or oversize—as long as the batter is mounded slightly above the lip and you adjust the cooking time to fit the size of the cups. But if you like domed tops and beautiful edges, look for a 24-cup pan, or use two 12-cup tins.

Yes, I use my ice cream scoop for ice cream, but not as much as I use it for other things. I actually have a whole collection of ice cream scoops, sturdy metal oval ones with a mechanical sweep built into them so that contents come out easily and neatly. I use them to fill muffin tins, to scoop cookie dough, and to spoon pancake and waffle batter. The ice cream scoops allow me to work quickly and precisely.

A spatula is important for all cooking, but particularly for baking, when you're constantly scraping down the sides of a mixer or scooping batters out of bowls. I like spatulas with firm plastic handles and heatproof rubber, so that you don't have to worry about melting or burning if you accidentally leave the spatula on the edge of a pot. Having a sturdy spatula makes all the difference—you don't want one with a wooden handle and a detachable rubber end, as food can get stuck in the end and (since it's detachable) it obviously has a tendency to come off.

Do you absolutely need one of these? No. But they're super handy and take up a lot less space than a standing blender, so if you don't have a lot of room, you might want to consider getting one of these. Immersion blenders are great for blending and puréeing mixtures that are already in pots, like soups or stewed fruit. They're also useful for blending small amounts, as you can put the blender wand right into a cup or bowl (make sure it has high sides) and mix the contents then and there. I use mine for blending crêpe batter and for most of the fruit purées and butters that I use to sweeten the cakes and batters in this book.

Ice Cream Scoop

Heatproof Spatula

Immersion Blender

Pantry

Work with your **pantry**, and **learn** from the **results**— that's how many of **the recipes** in **this book** were **developed**.

You get up on a Sunday morning and you want to bake something but find you don't have all the ingredients. You forgot a certain flour, you've run out of whole milk, you can't find the nutmeg, your kids ate the last ripe peach. The farmers' market is open, but you're in your pajamas. Or maybe you don't have the luxury of living near a farmers' market or an upscale grocery store might be too pricy.

This is an opportunity to use your imagination. Look around your pantry, check your refrigerator, and use what you have. Swap ingredients. Improvise. Recipes are meant to be roadmaps, diagrams, records of inspiration and experimentation on the parts of the cooks who wrote them.

That said, it *is* important to figure out what you can change in a recipe and what you can't. Baking soda and baking powder, for instance, are not interchangeable. Full-fat dairy products behave differently from nonfat or lowfat ones. Salt is there for a reason, as is a specific quantity of flour, butter, or sugar. Most types of fruits and nuts are interchangeable, as are many herbs, spices, and chocolates. If you don't have buttermilk, substitute the same amount with part milk and part yogurt. If you don't have apples, use pears, but change the cinnamon to nutmeg or toss in a few cloves. If you don't have barley flour, try the recipe with rye flour.

Work with your pantry, and learn from the results—that's how many of the recipes in this book were developed. The Pear and Buckwheat Pancakes (see page 79) started out as applesauce pancakes, until I ran out of applesauce and reached for the ripe pears on my counter.

Following is a list of staples that will keep your pantry well stocked and ready to get baking.

Flour

Since whole-grain flours are milled from the entire grain—bran, endosperm, and germ—they have a higher oil content than other flours and are therefore more inclined to go rancid. As I use my flours so much, I keep them on my counter, in glass jars screwed tightly shut, so that I have easy access to them. If you don't bake frequently, flours should be stored in the refrigerator in separate, sealed containers. I don't store flour in the freezer, as I find that it picks up off flavors.

A note about flour mites: They can eat through plastic bags—yet another reason for storing flours in separate, sealed containers. That way if you do have an infestation, the bugs will be contained and only that one flour will need to be thrown away. My mom taught me to kill flour mites by freezing a bag of flour for three days before storing it.

Vanilla

Vanilla beans are expensive, but they're worth it when used in custards or jams. The flavors of Mexican, Tahitian, and Bourbon-Madagascar vanilla beans are phenomenal, and the seeds scraped from the beans are lovely in recipes, the tiny flecks signaling that you've used the real thing. To keep them from drying out, store vanilla beans in a sealed container in the refrigerator or the freezer. (At Spago we stored whole vanilla beans in huge jars of vanilla extract, which would plump up the beans and infuse the extract with even more flavor.) If you don't have vanilla beans, substituting pure vanilla extract is an option, though the flavor won't be as intense as that of the vanilla beans. I use pure vanilla extract for cookie doughs and muffin or cake batters.

Spices

Most of us have collections of spice jars, from past experiments or that we picked up out of habit, forgetting that we still had some at home. They mostly sit on the shelf, unused, sometimes for years. But spices have a shelf life; they grow stale or rancid, and they lose their flavor. Fresh spices can make an incredible difference in a recipe. Use a permanent marker and date your jars. Every year, update your spice rack and trade old jars for new ones. Also bear in mind that some spices are worth purchasing whole. Ground nutmeg, for example, tastes like dust when you compare it to freshly grated. Purchased ground cumin pales in comparison to freshly toasted and ground whole seeds. Cardamom is far more flavorful (and less expensive, especially if you get it in an Indian, Asian or Mexican market) when you buy whole pods. Where applicable, toast spices before you use them and grind them yourself in a spice (or pepper or coffee) grinder. If you have access to a co-op or a store with bulk bins, buy your spices there, as you can buy just what you need for much less money.

Butter

I always bake with unsalted butter, and all the recipes in this book call for it because it allows you to control the amount of salt in your recipe. Specialty butters like Plugra, which are sometimes labeled "European-style," can be used in any of these recipes, if you want to spend the extra money. Use specialty butter in recipes where it will have the most impact, like pie crust, cookies, biscuits, and scones. Vegetable shortening also has its place in pastry—see Spelt Pie Dough (page 163)—but for pure flavor, nothing takes the place of butter.

Salt

Salt is just as important in baking as it is in savory cooking. It can bring out the nuanced flavors of chocolate, add depth to fruits, and brighten elements of any dessert. So when a recipe calls for a specific measurement of salt, don't ignore it—measure that amount into your bowl or pan. Your recipe will be the better for it.

My recipes call for kosher salt, which is larger-grained than many types of common salt. I like the occasional hint of salt you get when you bite into baked goods made with it, especially cookies. You can substitute sea salt or any common table salt you have on hand, but you'll need to adjust the amount you use, because sea salt weighs twice as much as an equal measure of kosher salt. (I use Diamond Crystal kosher salt, which is finer-grade than many kosher salts on the market.) Food scientist and cookbook author Shirley Corriher uses this formula: 1 tablespoon of table or sea salt = 1½ tablespoons Morton kosher salt = 2 tablespoons Diamond Crystal kosher salt.

Chocolate

The kind of chocolate you bake with—a favorite milk chocolate or a bar of 73-percent cacao from Venezuela—will largely determine your finished product. My favorite has always been Valrhona, a French chocolate that has smoothness and depth and also melts very easily. In recent years, there's been a huge increase in the number of artisanal chocolate makers, with many small chocolatiers sourcing cacao beans at origin and making their own chocolate by hand in small batches, using the best quality ingredients. But specialty chocolate can be very expensive. There is a world of chocolate out there and determining what kind you use is a deeply personal choice. I often pair a more bitter chocolate (one with a high percentage of cacao) with recipes that are already sweet, so as not to make them more so.

Dairy is an essential component in baking—not just butter, but also cream, milk, yogurt, and buttermilk. All of the dairy called for in my recipes is full-fat as I like the flavor of full-fat products and my recipes are designed for them. You may substitute lowfat or nonfat products, but take into consideration that your results will differ due to the change in overall fat content. I prefer to use organic dairy products, but if you don't have them or don't want to pay the higher price, it won't affect the outcome of the recipes. Yogurt is added in some recipes for flavor, texture, and thickness, or to cut down on the amount of butter used. Yogurt and buttermilk both have a slight tang and acidity that I really like.

Many of my recipes call for "sugar," by which I mean standard white granulated sugar. If other sweeteners are also called for, I've gravitated toward darker and more full-bodied ones. Darker sugars tend to enhance the flavors of many of the flours used in this book, particularly those with assertive profiles. The molasses I use is unsulphured and not blackstrap. When using honey, I usually use a mild one, like orange-blossom. But in recipes that use more intense flours such as amaranth, whole-wheat, or teff, you might experiment with a specialty honey, like chestnut, linden, or sage.

I use large-grade eggs, preferably organic. I always take my eggs straight from the refrigerator. Using cold eggs doesn't seem to affect most recipes unless they call for whipping egg whites, which get more volume if they're brought to room temperature first. If you prefer baking with room-temperature eggs, they also work just fine. A quick trick for warming eggs up quickly is to set them into a bowl of hot water.

Dairy

Sweeteners

Eggs

whole wheat

The shift to whole-grain baking usually begins with plain whole-wheat flour, the most commonly used whole-grain flour in home and professional kitchens. There is often a moment when measuring cups of all-purpose flour are traded for cups of whole-wheat—perhaps gradually, perhaps all at once. This is frequently part of a search for healthier alternatives, or it may be an impulse to add more flavor to dough or cookie batter. In my experience, it was a little of both.

If you've already made this transition to whole-grain baking, now the questions are how much, what kind, how far to take the flavors. Tear open a bag of freshly milled whole-wheat flour, sift it with your hands, and smell the profound difference between this and the standard all-purpose flour that is the workhorse of most kitchens. Whole-wheat is nutty, earthy, with hints of caramel and brown sugar, and it has a depth that brings out the flavors of the ingredients you pair it with—it matches equally well with the fruit and chocolate in many desserts, and the cheeses, spices, and herbs in savory recipes.

While all-purpose flour is milled from wheat that has had some or all of the germ and bran removed, whole-wheat flour is, by definition, ground from the entire wheat berry. It has a mottled, pale-brown color with flecks of the entire grain sifted throughout, a distinctly nutty taste, and a grainy texture. Some whole-wheat flour can be quite assertive, with a strong, earthy flavor that may have a bitter edge. This bitterness comes from the phenolic acid present in the bran, which can give the flour a slight tannic aftertaste, rather like red wine.

Since all whole-grain flour has a higher oil content than refined flour, it can turn rancid more easily—so always check the milling date on the flour and store it properly (see page 32).

Even if you love the flavor of whole-wheat flour, it's often helpful to blend it with other wheat flours—usually all-purpose, or even some other types, like spelt or Kamut. This tempers the flavor and balances the structure of a pastry. Whole-wheat flour can be quite heavy and can create a very dense loaf or batter; blending in lighter wheat flours can provide the lift and airy crumb you want, without compromising the characteristics of the whole wheat.

Whole-wheat flours can vary quite a lot, depending on the type of wheat milled for the flour—there are thousands of varieties of wheat and at least a hundred grown in this heavily wheat-producing country alone. Most whole-wheat flour is milled from hard red wheat, which can be either a spring or a winter variety. With the growing interest in whole grains, there are also other whole-wheat flours making their way into markets. White whole-wheat flour—a softer, lighter, albino strain made from a variety of white wheats—is now easy to find. Other specialty wheat flours like emmer, spelt, and Kamut are also becoming more readily available.

Graham flour is another option, and one I use in this book for a version of graham crackers. It was named for a nineteenth-century American Presbyterian minister, Reverend Sylvester Graham, who was an early advocate of whole-wheat flour. Graham flour is simply a coarsely ground whole-wheat flour.

There are also other types of wheat flours that are frequently used in baking: bread flour, similar to all-purpose but with a higher protein content; pastry flour, with a lower protein content and a finer, almost clumpy consistency; and cake flour, which is bleached, very finely powdered and has an even lower protein content than pastry flour. For the recipes in this book, I sometimes

There are also **other types of wheat flours** that are frequently used in baking: **bread flour**, **pastry flour**, and **cake flour**. Whichever mixture you use, **wheat flours** are the **foundation** of my kitchen.

call for whole-grain pastry flour, which is made of softer wheat than whole-wheat flour and is more finely ground. I've found that it balances the harder, coarser whole-wheat flour and makes for a finer crumb.

Whichever mixture you use, wheat flours are the foundation of my kitchen. Figuring out how they work to give pastries their structure and flavor is at the heart of this book. Wheat flours form the basis of the recipes not only in this chapter but in the ones that follow as well, as other whole-grain recipes often require the addition of all-purpose flour to give them the desired rise and structure.

Chocolate Chip **Cookies**

These cookies are the size of your palm, with thick, chewy edges, soft centers, and big chocolate chunks. It's surprising just how delicious this whole-wheat version of an old classic is. Unlike many of the recipes in this book, this cookie is made with 100 percent whole-wheat flour, which gives it a distinctive, nutty taste. Use a good bittersweet chocolate for these cookies, as the flavor of high-quality chocolate pairs best with whole-wheat flour.

1. Place two racks in the upper and lower thirds of the oven and preheat to 350°F. Line two baking sheets with parchment. Although you can butter the sheets instead, parchment is useful for these cookies because the large chunks of chocolate can stick to the pan.

2. Sift the dry ingredients into a large bowl, pouring back into the bowl any bits of grain or other ingredients that may remain in the sifter.

3. Add the butter and the sugars to the bowl of a standing mixer fitted with a paddle attachment. With the mixer on low speed, mix just until the butter and sugars are blended, about 2 minutes. Use a spatula to scrape down the sides of the bowl. Add the eggs one at a time, mixing until each is combined. Mix in the vanilla. Add the flour mixture to the bowl and blend on low speed until the flour is barely combined, about 30 seconds. Scrape down the sides and bottom of the bowl.

4. Add the chocolate all at once to the batter. Mix on low speed until the chocolate is evenly combined. Use a spatula to scrape down the sides and bottom of the bowl, then scrape the batter out onto a work surface, and use your hands to fully incorporate all the ingredients (see Sidebar, page 142).

5. Scoop mounds of dough about 3 tablespoons in size onto the baking sheet, leaving 3 inches between them, or about 6 to a sheet.

6. Bake the cookies for 16 to 20 minutes, rotating the sheets halfway through, until the cookies are evenly dark brown. Transfer the cookies, still on the parchment, to the counter to cool, and repeat with the remaining dough. These cookies are best eaten warm from the oven or later that same day. They'll keep in an airtight container for up to 3 days.

Parchment for the baking sheets

DRY MIX:

3 cups whole-wheat flour

$1^1/2$ teaspoons baking powder

1 teaspoon baking soda

$1^1/2$ teaspoons kosher salt

WET MIX:

8 ounces (2 sticks) cold unsalted butter, cut into $1/2$-inch pieces

1 cup dark brown sugar

1 cup sugar

2 eggs

2 teaspoons pure vanilla extract

8 ounces bittersweet chocolate, roughly chopped into $1/4$- and $1/2$-inch pieces

Note: This dough is made to go straight from the bowl into the oven. However, for freshly baked cookies anytime, you can refrigerate some of the dough for later. Be sure to scoop out the balls of dough before chilling, as the cold dough is too difficult to scoop (see page 30 for Sherry Yard's technique on rolling cookie dough into logs). Also, remember that cookies baked from chilled dough will be thicker than those made from room-temperature dough. This dough—scooped, chilled, and wrapped in plastic—will last in the refrigerator for one week—assuming it doesn't get eaten first!

Drop Biscuits with **Strawberries** and **Cream**

SERVES 6

Butter for the baking sheet

BISCUITS:

¾ cup whole-wheat flour

¾ cup all-purpose flour

¼ cup sugar

2 teaspoons baking powder

¼ teaspoon kosher salt

1 cup cold heavy cream

FINISH:

1½ teaspoons sugar for
    dusting

1 pound strawberries, hulled
    and sliced

1 tablespoon sugar

1 cup cold heavy cream

⅓ cup crème fraîche,
    optional

My great-grandmother would make drop biscuits for me every summer when I was growing up. Hers were made from a boxed mix, sprinkled with sugar, and served with sliced sugared strawberries and a generous dollop of Cool Whip. I just loved sitting out on her back porch way past bedtime, in the summer heat, eating biscuits with her. This recipe is my updated version, composed around whole-wheat flour. Drop a warm biscuit into a bowl with some unsweetened whipped cream and a large spoonful of macerated fresh strawberries. It's every bit as good as my great-grandmother's dessert, just without the extra sugar and additives.

1. Position a rack in the middle of the oven and preheat to 325°F. Rub a baking sheet lightly with butter.
2. In a large bowl, sift together the flours, sugar, baking powder, and salt, pouring back into the bowl any bits of grain or other ingredients that may remain in the sifter.
3. Pour in the cream and, using a fork or your hands, stir until the dough just begins to come together. The dough will be very shaggy; do not overmix.

4. Pile the dough into six mounds, leaving 4 inches between them. Use your hands to tuck in the rough pieces of the dough. Sprinkle the biscuits with the remaining 1½ teaspoons of sugar.
5. Bake the biscuits for 34 to 40 minutes, rotating the sheet once halfway through, until they begin to color on the top.
6. While the biscuits are baking, place the berries in a bowl and toss with 1 tablespoon of sugar. Allow them to macerate, uncovered at room temperature, for about 30 minutes, or until the biscuits are done. Meanwhile, whip the remaining cup of cream (combined with crème fraîche, if desired— see Sidebar) into soft peaks that barely hold their shape, and chill.
7. When the biscuits are out of the oven, fill six bowls with cream and berries, then nestle a warm biscuit alongside.

Whipped Cream

Whipped cream should always be softly whipped, without distinct peaks, and never cracked or broken. One way to achieve this is to add crème fraîche to the whipping cream, usually a third of the amount as there is cream. Crème fraîche gives a little tang while providing body and keeping the cream from overwhipping. It takes longer to whip, and the resulting cream has more gloss, is creamier than plain whipped cream, and spoons softly.

42   GOOD TO THE GRAIN

Gingersnaps

This is a spiced cookie, great for holiday dessert tables and gift boxes. With a cracked surface, chewy edges, and a sparkly sugar crust, this cookie gets spice and heat from freshly grated ginger. Its cracked surface is the result of a large amount of sugar, which is offset by the assertive whole-wheat flour. The texture—whether crispy or chewy—depends on how long the cookies are baked, so you can adjust the baking time to your preference.

1. In a large bowl, mix together the melted butter, sugars, molasses, ginger, and egg. Sift the dry ingredients over the butter-sugar mixture, pouring back into the bowl any bits of grain or other ingredients that may remain in the sifter, and stir to form a batter. Wrap the dough in plastic wrap and chill for at least 2 hours, or preferably overnight.

2. Position two racks in the upper and lower thirds of the oven and preheat to 350°F. Rub two baking sheets lightly with butter. Pour ½ cup of sugar into a shallow bowl.

3. Pluck out balls of dough about 1 tablespoon in size, toss them in the sugar, roll them into balls, and toss the balls back into the sugar for a second coating until they are sparkly white. Place the balls on the baking sheets, leaving about 2 inches between them. Repeat with the remaining dough. The balls of dough that don't fit on this round of baking can be double dipped in the sugar and chilled.

4. Bake for 10 to 15 minutes, rotating the pan halfway through, until the color is dark and even all the way across the cookie. Remove the cookies from the oven, slide a thin metal spatula under each of them, and transfer them to a baking rack.

5. Repeat with the remaining dough.

6. These cookies are best eaten warm from the oven or later that same day. They'll keep in an airtight container for up to 3 days.

Butter for the baking sheets

WET MIX:

4 ounces (1 stick) unsalted butter, melted and cooled slightly

½ cup dark brown sugar

½ cup sugar

¼ cup unsulphured (not blackstrap) molasses

2 tablespoons grated fresh ginger, from about a 2½-inch piece

1 egg

DRY MIX:

1 cup whole-wheat flour

1 cup all-purpose flour

2 teaspoons baking soda

½ teaspoon ginger

¼ teaspoon cinnamon

⅛ teaspoon clove

½ teaspoon kosher salt

FINISH:

½ cup sugar

Sweet Potato **Muffins**

2 small sweet potatoes or
one medium sweet potato,
about ³/₄ pound total
Butter for the tins

DRY MIX:
1 cup whole-wheat flour
1 cup all-purpose flour
1 tablespoon cinnamon
1 teaspoon baking powder
¹/₂ teaspoon baking soda
¹/₂ teaspoon kosher salt
¹/₂ teaspoon nutmeg, freshly
grated
¹/₄ teaspoon allspice

WET MIX:
2 ounces (¹/₂ stick) cold
unsalted butter
¹/₄ cup sugar
¹/₄ cup dark brown sugar
1 egg
1 cup buttermilk
¹/₂ cup plain yogurt
6 large Medjool dates, pitted
and finely chopped

The trick to making muffins with cooked fruit and vegetables is having tasty leftovers on hand. My kids love roasted sweet potatoes, so I always make a little extra to stir into a muffin or pancake batter. If you don't have that kind of production going on in your kitchen, throw a tray of sweet potatoes into the oven the next time you're baking, or roast extra with a recipe and refrigerate or freeze the leftovers. Roast the potatoes until they're very dark, even burning slightly around the edges. It might seem like you're taking them too far, but this caramelization gives them more flavor.

1. Preheat the oven to 400°F. Line a baking sheet with parchment or aluminum foil and roast the sweet potatoes for 1 to 1¹/₂ hours, depending on their size, until they're tender when pierced with a fork. The bottoms should be dark, even burnt-looking, and the juices beginning to caramelize. Set aside to cool, then peel and leave whole.

2. Lower the oven to 350°F. Rub muffin tins with a ¹/₃-cup capacity with butter.

3. Sift the dry ingredients into a large bowl, pouring back into the bowl any bits of grain or other ingredients that may remain in the sifter. In a small bowl, whisk together the buttermilk and yogurt.

4. Add the butter and the sugars to the bowl of a standing mixer. Attach the paddle and mix on high speed until the butter and sugars are light and creamy, about 3 minutes. Using a spatula, scrape down the sides of the bowl. Add the egg and half of the sweet potatoes and mix on medium speed for about 1 minute, until thoroughly combined. Again, scrape down the sides of the bowl.

5. On low speed, so that the flour doesn't go flying everywhere, add the dry ingredients and mix until partly combined. Add the buttermilk mixture and mix until combined. Add the

chopped dates, separating them over the surface of the batter so they don't clump together. Add the remaining sweet potatoes and mix until barely combined; there should be pockets of sweet potato in the batter. Use a spatula to scrape down the sides and bottom of the bowl.

6. Scoop the batter into 10 muffin cups, using a spoon or an ice cream scoop. The batter should be slightly mounded above the edge.

7. Bake for 35 to 40 minutes, rotating the pans halfway through. The muffins are ready when their bottoms are dark golden in color (twist a muffin out of the pan to check). Take the tins out of the oven, twist each muffin out, and place it on its side in the cup to cool. This ensures that the muffin stays crusty instead of getting soggy. These muffins are best eaten warm from the oven or later that same day. They can also be kept in an airtight container for up to 2 days, or frozen and reheated.

Coffee Cake

All the muffin recipes in this book can double as coffee cakes. This is handy if you don't have a muffin tin, or if you find a recipe that you really like and want to bake it into a different form. Prepare the batter as instructed, but instead of scooping it into individual muffin cups, spread the batter into a 9- or 10-inch cake pan or a bread loaf pan. If there is a topping, just add it to the top as you would with the muffin recipe. Bake the cake or bread for 45 minutes to 1 hour, and take it out when it's done (test the center with a skewer).

Note: To encourage even baking and to allow each muffin enough room to have an individual dome top, fill alternate cups in a 24-cup tin, or use two 12-cup tins.

Apple Graham Coffee Cake

Butter for the pan

APPLE TOPPING:
2 large tart apples
1 ounce (¹/₄ stick) unsalted
    butter
2 tablespoons sugar
1 teaspoon cinnamon

DRY MIX:
³/₄ cup all-purpose flour
³/₄ cup graham flour
³/₄ cup whole-grain pastry
    flour
¹/₃ cup sugar
¹/₃ cup dark brown sugar
1 teaspoon baking powder
¹/₂ teaspoon baking soda
1 tablespoon cinnamon
1 teaspoon ground ginger
1 teaspoon kosher salt

WET MIX:
2 ounces (¹/₂ stick) unsalted
    butter, melted and cooled
    slightly
1 cup buttermilk
¹/₄ cup whole plain yogurt
¹/₄ cup unsweetened
    applesauce
1 egg

This is my coffee cake recipe for leisurely weekend baking. There are three kinds of flour in this batter, each one playing a different role. The graham flour adds flavor and a fine sandiness, while the all-purpose flour lightens the graham flour. The whole-grain pastry flour gives the cake its tender crumb. Caramelizing the apples concentrates the flavor of the fruit. You can use any apples you have on hand, but tart cooking apples like Granny Smiths work best, as their acidity offsets the richness of the butter and sugar, and they're firm enough to withstand the caramelizing. In the time it takes to cook the apples, the coffee cake can be stirred together.

1. Place a rack in the middle of the oven and preheat to 350°F. Rub a 9-inch round pan with high (2¹/₂-inch) sides with butter.

2. Peel the apples, then quarter and core them. Cut each quarter into thirds, then slice into pieces as thick as your thumb. They'll be candy-corn-shaped, and will make a nice rustic topping for the cake.

3. Melt the ounce of butter, the sugar, and the cinnamon in a 12-inch skillet over medium-high heat until bubbly. (If you don't have a large enough skillet, sauté the apples in two batches.) Add the apples and toss to coat them with the butter mixture, and let the apples sear for 1 minute without stirring. Cook for 6 to 10 minutes, until tender and caramelized, stirring every minute or so. In order to get color on the apples, it is important that they are tossed, left to sit for a minute, then tossed again and left to sit. As the apples cook, they will become soft and caramelized around the edges and smell like an apple pie baking.

4. Remove the caramelized apples from the heat before they become dry; scrape them onto a plate along with any buttery sauce. You will add this later as a topping.

5. Sift the dry ingredients into a large bowl, pouring back into the bowl any bits of grain or other ingredients that may remain in the sifter, and set aside.

6. Whisk together the wet ingredients until thoroughly combined. Using a spatula, scrape the wet ingredients into the dry ones and gently mix together. Scrape the batter into the buttered pan, smooth the top with the spatula, and top with the caramelized apples, evenly spreading them to the edges.

7. Bake on the middle rack for 40 to 48 minutes, rotating the pan halfway through. The cake is ready when it is golden brown and springs back when lightly touched, or when a skewer inserted in the center comes out clean. The cake can be eaten warm from the pan, or cooled, wrapped tightly in plastic, and kept for up to 2 days.

Blue **Cheese** and **Onion Scones**

For these scones, nutty graham flour is paired with all-purpose flour, rich blue cheese, and caramelized onions. Sweetened slightly with honey but still definitely savory, they are a great accompaniment for a green salad or a cheese plate. Graham flour gives these scones a distinctly coarse texture, more so than a regular whole-wheat flour would, although you can substitute whole-wheat flour for graham flour. The Onion Jam yields twice as much as you need here; you can either double the scone recipe or save the onions for another use.

Parchment for the baking
sheets

DRY MIX:

$1^{1}/_{2}$ cups graham flour

$1^{1}/_{4}$ cups all-purpose flour

2 tablespoons sugar

2 teaspoons baking powder

1 teaspoon baking soda

$^{3}/_{4}$ teaspoon kosher salt

WET MIX:

4 ounces (1 stick) cold
unsalted butter

4 ounces blue cheese,
crumbled

1 cup buttermilk

$^{1}/_{2}$ cup Onion Jam, or half a
batch (see page 189)

$^{1}/_{4}$ cup honey

1. Place two racks in the upper and lower thirds of the oven and preheat to 375°F. Line two baking sheets with parchment.
2. Pull out a ruler and set it near where you're working; you'll use it later for measuring rectangles of dough.
3. Sift the dry ingredients into a large bowl, pouring back into the bowl any bits of grain or other ingredients that may remain in the sifter.
4. Cut the butter into $^{1}/_{4}$-inch pieces and add them to the dry mixture. Rub the butter pieces between your fingers, breaking them into smaller bits. Continue rubbing until the butter is in small pieces varying in size from rice grains to flattened peas. The more quickly you do this, the more the butter will stay solid, which is important for the success of the recipe. Stir the blue cheese into the dry mixture.
5. In a small bowl, whisk together the buttermilk, onion jam, and honey. Using a spatula, add the wet ingredients to the dry ingredients and gently combine.
6. Use a pastry scraper or spatula to get the dough onto a well-floured surface. If the dough is sticky, flour it and knead it together three times until a soft ball can be formed. The dough should be dry enough that it can be moved around on the counter and patted down without sticking, yet moist enough that the knife will be sticky when the dough is being cut into squares. Flour your hands and pat the dough into a rectangle. With a rolling pin, roll the dough into a rectangle that is about $7^{1}/_{2}$ inches by 9 inches and about 1 inch thick, flouring the work surface, the rolling pin, and your hands as needed.
7. Use a sharp knife to slice the rectangle into quarters both lengthwise and crosswise, making 16 rectangular scones, each about $2^{1}/_{4}$ inches by 2 inches. Place the scones a few inches apart on the parchment-lined baking sheets. (The scones can also be kept, covered, in the refrigerator and baked in the next 2 days.)
8. Bake the scones for 22 to 24 minutes, rotating the sheets halfway through. The scones are ready when their tops are golden brown and cheese has oozed out and begun to caramelize on the baking sheets. They are best eaten warm from the oven or later that same day.

Graham Nuts

Butter for the pan

DRY MIX:

1 cup graham flour

1/3 cup whole-wheat flour

1/3 cup dark brown sugar

1/2 teaspoon baking soda

1/2 teaspoon kosher salt

WET MIX:

1 cup buttermilk

1 tablespoon honey

1 teaspoon pure vanilla
extract

There's a special satisfaction I get when I manage to replicate at home something I've only ever found in a store. So I was very intrigued when I came across a recipe for homemade Grape Nuts, a crunchy, wholesome breakfast cereal, in an Amish cookbook, *Cooking from Quilt Country* by Marcia Adams. I never imagined that this commercial cereal had originated in home kitchens. A blend of graham and whole-wheat flours gives this cereal a tender yet nubby bite, and honey provides a touch of sweetness. I've altered Adams' recipe, but am indebted to her for the inspiration.

1. Position a rack in the middle of the oven and preheat to 350°F. Rub a baking sheet lightly with butter.
2. Sift the dry ingredients into a large bowl, pouring back into the bowl any bits of grain and other ingredients that may remain in the sifter, and set aside.
3. In a small bowl, mix together the buttermilk, honey, and vanilla. Add the wet ingredients to the dry ingredients and mix together with a spatula to form a batter.
4. Scrape the batter onto the baking sheet and, using the spatula or a metal offset spatula, spread the batter evenly across the entire surface of the sheet. The more evenly the batter is spread, the more evenly the cracker will bake—if you have a long, thin offset cake spatula, this is the time to use it.
5. Bake for 30 minutes, rotating the pan halfway through. Remove the baking sheet from the oven and break off any areas of the cracker that are getting dark or dry, and set them on a rack to cool.

Turn the oven down to 250°F, return the baking sheet to the oven, and bake for 55 to 60 minutes more. Every 20 minutes, break off any more dry sections and put them on the cooling rack. While you are doing this, break up the rest of the dough into smaller pieces to encourage the dough to dry out faster, and return the baking sheet to the oven for the remaining time.

6. Remove the sheet from the oven when the cracker is mahogany brown and entirely dry. Let all the pieces of the cracker cool on a rack.
7. Set up a food processor with a large-hole grater attachment. Feed pieces of the cracker through the tube at the top and grind into nuts. Serve with a pitcher of ice-cold milk. The graham nuts will store in an airtight jar for one month.

amaranth

Drop a handful of amaranth flour into a bowl and you'll see a finely ground powder that's the color of beach sand, pale beige with a hint of yellow. Its fragrance is strong and unique, grassy with subtle undertones of chalk or stone, more like hay than a freshly mown lawn. Frankly, it can be off-putting at first, but it mellows nicely when paired with other equally bold flavors.

Despite its grassiness, amaranth is neither a grass nor a cereal grain but a leafy and often very colorful plant prized as much for its edible greenery as for its abundant seeds. It's those seeds—a single amaranth plant is capable of producing about 50,000 of them—that are ground to make the flour.

Despite being used in this country primarily as a specialty flour, amaranth has a long, politically fraught history. The Aztec empire was built on amaranth. It was the principal crop of that Mesoamerican civilization four to six thousand years ago, before the arrival of the Spanish

Despite being used in this country **primarily** as **a specialty flour**, amaranth has a long, **politically fraught history**.

conquistadors. The Aztecs used both the leaves and the seeds of the plant, grinding the seeds into flour. Hernán Cortés and his army destroyed the crops during their conquest, deliberately burning the amaranth in particular. One of the uses the Aztecs had for amaranth flour was to mix it with honey to make little shaped cakes, some of which were said to contain human blood, for ritual sacrifices. Cortés thought that eradicating the amaranth might put an end to these pagan practices.

Amaranth has enjoyed a resurgence since the days when it was burned and banned by the Spanish, and it is now cultivated worldwide and valued for its high nutritional content. Its seeds are gluten-free and high in protein, lysine, and fiber, so the flour ground from them is useful for people with wheat allergies or gluten intolerance.

Developing recipes with amaranth was challenging. Some people find the assertive grassiness of the flour a bit overwhelming. Amaranth flour pairs very well with strong-flavored sweeteners like honey, molasses, and muscovado sugar, as they temper the boldness of the flour without masking its flavor. It's no accident that the recipes in this chapter rely heavily on these sweeteners—you'll find them in the Molasses Bran Muffins, Muscovado Sugar Cake, and Honey Hazelnut Cookies, which were inspired by the Aztecs' honey cakes. Finely ground nuts are a nice flavor fit, as are pungent spices.

Because of the lack of gluten in amaranth, I mix the flour with wheat flours or rising agents to get structure and height. Mixing amaranth with other flours also helps balance its strong flavor.

Developing recipes with amaranth **was challenging.** Amaranth flour **pairs very well** with **strong-flavored** sweeteners like **honey**, **molasses**, and **muscovado sugar**, as they **temper the boldness** of the flour **without masking** its flavor.

If you're new to amaranth flour and the grassiness is a bit too much for you, try substituting quinoa flour for the amaranth flour. Quinoa flour is similar in taste and quality—it's also distinctively grassy, very high in protein, and gluten-free—but its flavor is more muted.

It's fitting that the name "amaranth" comes from the Greek word for "unyielding" or "not withering." It's sometimes even translated as "immortal"—something Cortés probably wouldn't have appreciated.

Molasses Bran **Muffins**

MAKES 10 MUFFINS

Butter for the tins

1 cup orange juice, about
    3 oranges
1$\frac{1}{2}$ cups pitted prunes

DRY MIX:
1$\frac{1}{2}$ cups wheat bran
$\frac{1}{2}$ cup amaranth flour
1$\frac{1}{2}$ cups whole-wheat flour
2 tablespoons dark brown
    sugar
1$\frac{1}{4}$ teaspoons baking soda
$\frac{1}{2}$ teaspoon kosher salt
$\frac{1}{2}$ teaspoon cinnamon

WET MIX:
2 cups buttermilk
$\frac{1}{2}$ cup molasses
3 tablespoons unsalted
    butter, melted and cooled
    slightly
1 egg
1 tablespoon orange zest,
    from the oranges used for
    juice

Bran muffins can be a world better than the tasteless "healthy" muffins you often find in stores. This muffin is laced with orange, spice, and a prune purée that lends moisture as well as tartness. The muffins taste great once cooled, and they're even better a day or two later, after the flavors have had some time to come together. This recipe makes more prune purée than you need for the muffins. Keep the extra frozen or chilled to use as a great spread on toast or in plain yogurt—or for making more muffins.

1. To make the prune jam, bring the orange juice and the prunes to a boil in a small saucepan. Turn the flame off, cover, and let steep until the prunes are plump and have absorbed some of the juice, about 30 minutes. Using an immersion blender, purée the prunes and juice in the pan until smooth.

2. Preheat the oven to 350°F. Rub muffin tins with a $\frac{1}{3}$-cup capacity with butter.

3. Measure the bran into a medium bowl. Warm the buttermilk over a gentle flame until just lukewarm. If the buttermilk is overheated it will separate, so don't leave the pan unattended.

4. Sift the dry ingredients into a large bowl, pouring back into the bowl any bits of grain or other ingredients that may remain in the sifter, and set aside.

5. In a small bowl, whisk the wet ingredients together with $\frac{1}{2}$ cup of the prune jam, making sure that the egg is thoroughly mixed in. Add this mixture to the softened bran, stir, then add the entire wet mixture to the dry mixture, stirring gently to form a batter.

6. Scoop the batter into 10 muffin cups, using a spoon or an ice cream scoop. The batter should be slightly mounded above the edge.

7. Bake for 30 to 34 minutes, rotating the pans halfway through. The muffins are ready to come out when their bottoms are a dark golden color (twist a muffin out of the pan to check). Take the tins out of the oven, twist each muffin out, and place it on its side in the cup to cool. This ensures that the muffin stays crusty instead of getting soggy. These muffins are best eaten once cooled. They can also be kept in an airtight container for up to 2 days, or frozen and reheated.

Note: To encourage even baking and to allow each muffin enough room to have an individual dome top, fill alternate cups in a 24-cup tin, or use two 12-cup tins.

Honey Amaranth **Waffles**

These waffles are sweetened with honey and made with both amaranth flour and flaxseed meal—all with robust flavors that complement each other and give the waffles their distinctive heartiness. Although most pancake and waffle batters are fine if they sit for a while before you griddle them, this batter needs to be used right away because the buttermilk and the baking soda begin to react as soon as they come into contact with each other. Because of the natural affinity of honey and yogurt, these waffles are fantastic served with a huge dollop of Greek yogurt.

1. Turn the waffle iron to its highest setting. Even if you don't usually heat it this high, these waffles come out best when cooked at high heat. Sift the dry ingredients into a large bowl, pouring back into the bowl any bits of grain or other ingredients that may remain in the sifter.
2. In a medium bowl, whisk together the wet ingredients until thoroughly combined. Using a spatula, add the wet ingredients to the dry ingredients and gently combine. The batter will begin to bubble and swell as the baking soda begins to react with the buttermilk.
3. Brush the waffle iron generously with butter; this is the key to a crisp crust. Use a ladle or measuring cup to scoop $1/2$ cup batter onto the spaces of the iron. Promptly close, and listen for the iron to sigh as the batter begins to cook. The smell wafting from the iron starts out like a freshly kneaded loaf of bread, then becomes toasty. Remove the waffle when the indicator light shows that it is done, or when a quick peek shows that it's turned a dark golden-brown, 4 to 6 minutes. Remove the hot waffle with a fork, and repeat with the remaining batter.
4. The waffles are best eaten right off the griddle, with a bit of butter, a drizzle of honey, or a hearty spoonful of Greek yogurt, as desired.

2 ounces ($1/2$ stick) unsalted butter, melted, for the waffle iron

DRY MIX:

$1/4$ cup amaranth flour

$1/4$ cup flaxseed meal

1 cup whole-wheat flour

1 cup all-purpose flour

2 tablespoons sugar

2 teaspoons baking powder

1 teaspoon baking soda

1 teaspoon kosher salt

WET MIX:

2 cups buttermilk

$1/4$ cup plus 2 tablespoons honey

2 eggs

2 tablespoons unsalted butter, melted and cooled slightly

FINISH:

Greek yogurt, optional

Honey Hazelnut **Cookies**

Butter for the pans
¹/₂ cup raw hazelnuts, skin on
4 ounces (1 stick) unsalted
   butter, softened to room
   temperature

DRY MIX:
¹/₄ cup amaranth flour
1 cup all-purpose flour
¹/₂ cup sugar
1¹/₂ teaspoons kosher salt

SYRUP:
¹/₄ cup honey
5 pods cardamom, smashed
Zest of 1 orange, using a wide
   peeler
1 tablespoon orange-blossom
   water

This crisp cookie is a cross between shortbread and linzer dough. It's a dry dough, crumbly and flecked with ground nuts. Two components tame the amaranth flour: the toasted hazelnuts, ground with their skins on for extra flavor and color, and honey, which is infused with orange peel, cardamom, and orange-blossom water before being brushed on the warm cookies. Open up your drawers and find your favorite cookie cutters—this is a fantastic dough for cutout shapes.

1. Place oven racks at the upper and lower thirds of the oven and preheat to 350°F. Spread the hazelnuts evenly on a baking sheet and toast them in the oven for 16 to 18 minutes, stirring halfway through, until the nuts are fragrant and dark brown but not burnt. Remove from the oven and cool. Once the nuts are cool, grind them, skins and all, in a food processor until finely ground, about 20 seconds.

2. Rub two baking sheets lightly with butter.

3. While the nuts are toasting, sift the dry ingredients into a bowl, pouring back any bits of grain or other ingredients that may remain in the sifter. Add the softened butter and the ground hazelnuts to the dry ingredients and rub the butter into the dough with your fingers. The ingredients should just barely come together. Dump the dough out onto a floured work surface and press it together.

4. Using a rolling pin, roll the dough out to a thickness of about ³/₁₆ inch. If the dough seems to be cracking, push it back into place and continue rolling. You probably won't need any additional flour to roll out the dough, as it will be quite dry. Using a

2-inch cookie cutter, cut the dough into circles and transfer them to the buttered baking sheets. Alternatively, you can use cookie cutters of any shape.

5. Bake for 20 to 24 minutes, depending on the size and shape of your cookies. Rotate the pan halfway through. The cookies should be evenly golden, with slightly darker edges and a dark golden bottom crust. When the cookies come out of the oven, move them onto a baking rack for glazing.

6. Meanwhile, make the syrup. In a small saucepan over a low flame, melt the honey, cardamom, orange zest, and orange-blossom water. Do not let the syrup boil, as you don't want to reduce the honey and risk crystallization. Stir the syrup and remove it from the heat, letting it infuse for a minimum of 15 minutes.

7. To glaze the cookies, brush each one twice while they are still warm to give the glaze a chance to soak into them. These cookies are best eaten as soon as they've cooled, but they'll keep in an airtight container for up to 3 days.

Muscovado Sugar Cake

Muscovado sugar is an unrefined brown sugar made from sugarcane juice, and has a stronger, more pungent taste than other brown sugars—many of which are just blends of refined white sugar and molasses. It's a great match for amaranth, because it stands up to the grain's grassy flavor. If you don't have or can't find muscovado sugar, regular dark brown sugar can be substituted. Apple butter, which is more concentrated than applesauce, adds richness and moisture. You can use either the Apple Butter recipe on page 198 or store-bought natural apple butter—or, in a pinch, substitute applesauce.

Butter for the pan

DRY MIX:
1/2 cup amaranth flour
1/2 cup whole-wheat flour
1/2 cup all-purpose flour
3/4 cup muscovado sugar
1 1/2 teaspoons baking powder
1/2 teaspoon kosher salt

WET MIX:
2 ounces (1/2 stick) cold unsalted butter, cut into 1/4-inch pieces
2 eggs, separated
1/2 cup whole milk
2 tablespoons Apple Butter (see page 198) or store-bought natural apple butter
1 tablespoon sugar

FINISH:
1 cup heavy cream
1/3 cup crème fraîche, optional

1. Position a rack in the middle of the oven and preheat to 350°F. Rub a 9-inch round cake pan lightly with butter.

2. Sift the dry ingredients into a large mixing bowl, pouring back into the bowl any grains or other ingredients that may remain in the sifter. Add the cubes of cold butter. Rub the butter between your fingers, breaking it into smaller and smaller bits, until it feels as coarse as cornmeal.

3. Place the egg whites into the bowl of a standing mixer fitted with a whip attachment and the yolks into a bowl large enough to hold the milk and apple butter. Whisk the egg yolks with the milk and apple butter until thoroughly combined. Scrape the milk mixture into the dry mixture with a spatula and stir to combine.

4. Whip the egg whites on the mixer's highest speed until they're softly whipped. Add the sugar and continue to mix until the whites are shiny and hold their peaks, about 1 minute. Use the spatula to scrape half of the whipped egg whites into the flour mixture and gently fold them in. Add the rest of the egg whites and gently fold them into the batter until the pockets of white have been incorporated. Scrape the batter into the pan, smoothing the top with the spatula.

5. Bake on the middle rack for 32 to 36 minutes, rotating the pan halfway through. The cake is ready when a light press in the middle causes it to spring back lightly and the edge of the cake is pulling away from the side of the pan.

6. Cool the cake in the pan. Once the cake is cool enough, slice it into wedges, whip the cream into soft peaks that barely hold their shape (see Sidebar, page 42), and dollop a spoonful over each wedge. Any leftover cake can be wrapped tightly in plastic and kept for up to 2 days.

Flatbread

Olive oil for the bowl

1 package active dry yeast

1 tablespoon honey

$1/2$ cup amaranth flour

3 cups all-purpose flour plus
extra for kneading and
dusting

1 tablespoon kosher salt

FINISH:

Olive oil for brushing

A pinch or two per flatbread
of dried oregano, dried
cumin, dried chile pepper,
sesame seeds, poppy seeds,
or other spices, to taste

Kosher or sea salt

This dough is supple, flavorful, and worth the wait of the rising time. If this is your first time making flatbread on the stove, watch for the small bubbles that pop up all over the surface just after the dough hits the hot pan—it's incredible. After the bread is flipped over to bake on the other side, those bubbles brown and crisp, adding crunch to the soft, chewy flatbread.

1. Lightly oil a large bowl to proof the dough in. Add $1^{1}/2$ cups warm water, yeast, and honey to a bowl. Stir together to combine, and allow the yeast to bloom for about 5 minutes, until it begins to bubble. (If it doesn't, it may be inactive; throw it out and start over with a new package.)

2. Add the flours and salt to the yeast mixture and stir to combine. Scrape the dough onto a generously floured surface and knead for about 5 minutes, adding up to $1/2$ cup of flour as needed to keep the dough from sticking, but not so much to dry it out. The dough should stay soft and tacky.

3. For the first rise, form the dough into a ball and place into the oiled bowl. Cover with a towel and allow to double in size, about 2 hours (see Sidebar, page 130).

4. For the second rise, fold the dough over itself, gently deflating it as you form it back into a ball. Arrange the dough so that the smooth side is facing up and cover with a towel. Let the dough rise for $1^{1}/2$ hours more.

5. After the second rise is done, scrape the dough onto a lightly floured work surface. Divide the dough into 8 equal pieces. Place a 10-inch cast-iron pan over medium heat.

6. Working with one piece of dough at a time on a generously floured surface, roll each piece into an irregular circle that will fit within the confines of the 10-inch pan— varying in thickness from $1/8$ to $1/4$ inch. Brush the top of the dough lightly with olive oil and dust with spices, herbs, or a mixture of both, and sprinkle with salt. Transfer the dough to the hot pan and grill, oiled side down, for 3 to 4 minutes. Moving the dough by hand from the counter to the pan requires patience; go slowly, lifting up around the edges and working toward the center until the entire flatbread is off the counter. With a quick and confident hand, move it to the pan to cook.

7. While the first side is griddling, brush the other side with oil and dust with more spices or herbs and salt. Flip the flatbread over and cook for another 2 to 3 minutes. Move the griddled flatbread to a baking rack. Repeat with the remaining pieces of dough, adjusting the heat and cooking time as you go to keep results consistent. Flatbreads are best when eaten right after they are griddled.

barley

Barley is by nature a workhorse, a grain with a long history of survival. Hardier than wheat or rye, barley has adapted over the millennia—evidence of cultivated barley dates back almost ten thousand years—and adjusted to the cultures and farming techniques of changing civilizations. It has been used as a cultivated crop, as medicine, as a form of measurement, even as currency. In modern times it's primarily used as animal feed, as malt for beer and whiskey-making, and as a sweetener.

The form of barley most commonly found in today's grocery stores is pearled barley, which has had not only the outer hull of the grain removed but also the bran. Pearled barley is delicious in soups and stews and can also be cooked into something resembling risotto. Toasting pearled barley before cooking enhances the grain's pure flavor and gives it a pleasant chewiness. Although it is less common, you can also find hulled barley, which has the bran still intact, and barley flakes,

Barley flour **isn't as common now** as it was **five hundred years ago**, when it was the **main bread grain** in Europe, before the tremendous rise of wheat.

in which hulled barley is processed like oatmeal. You can use hulled barley in place of the pearled barley in the recipe for Barley Porridge. Barley flakes are used in the Maple Pecan Granola.

Barley flour isn't as common now as it was five hundred years ago, when it was the main bread grain in Europe, before the tremendous rise of wheat. But its popularity is slowly growing again. Sifted into the dry ingredients of a recipe, barley flour has a soft texture that works really well in doughs and batters. With a scent that is strangely reminiscent of ripe apricots, barley flour is almost tart.

Because it has a lot of protein but not much gluten, barley is a great secondary flour, as in the Strawberry Scone and Bird Cracker recipes in this chapter. Paired with all-purpose flour, barley flour provides a boost of flavor, with the wheat flour making up the difference in structure and lift.

Strawberry Barley **Scones**

Barley flour has a distinctly sweet, creamy quality that tastes great with fruit. This recipe sandwiches a generous smear of jam between two disks of dough. When the scone bakes, the jam thickens, even caramelizing a little around the edges. Strawberry Jam (see page 190) is delightful in these scones, as is Three-Citrus Marmalade (see page 192), or you can use a purchased jam of your choice.

The moist dough and the small, irregular bits of butter are responsible for these tender scones. Resist the temptation to add more flour to the dough than you need—it should be sticky but manageable. A generously floured surface will help these scones come together.

Butter for the pan

DRY MIX:

1 cup plus 2 tablespoons
   barley flour

1 cup all-purpose flour

1/4 cup dark brown sugar

2 teaspoons baking powder

1/2 teaspoon baking soda

1 1/4 teaspoons kosher salt

WET MIX:

4 ounces (1 stick) cold
   unsalted butter

1/2 cup buttermilk

1 egg

FINISH:

1/2 cup Strawberry Jam (see
   page 190) or Three-Citrus
   Marmalade (see page 192)

1 tablespoon unsalted butter,
   melted

1 tablespoon sugar

1. Place a rack in the center of the oven and preheat to 350°F. Rub a baking sheet lightly with butter. Sift the dry ingredients into a large bowl, pouring back into the bowl any bits of grain or other ingredients that may remain in the sifter.

2. Cut the butter into 1/2-inch pieces and add them to the dry mixture. Use your hands to rub the butter between your fingers, breaking it into smaller bits. Continue rubbing until the butter is in sizes ranging from rice grains to flattened peas. The more quickly you do this, the more the butter will stay solid, which is important for the success of the recipe.

3. In a small bowl, whisk together the buttermilk and egg until thoroughly combined. Scrape the buttermilk and egg into the dry mixture, and mix until barely combined.

4. Use a pastry scraper or a spatula to transfer the dough onto a well-floured surface. The dough may be too sticky to handle; if it is, dust it with flour and fold it together a few times. Divide the

dough into 2 pieces. Flour your hands and pat each piece of dough into a disk about 3/4 inch thick and 7 inches in diameter.

5. Cover one disk with the jam or marmalade. Top the spread with the other disk and press down gently so that the dough settles into the jam. Brush the dough lightly with melted butter and sprinkle with sugar. Use a sharp knife to slice the circle into 8 triangular wedges, like a pie. Carefully place the wedges on the baking sheet, leaving a few inches between them.

6. Bake the scones for 22 to 26 minutes, rotating the sheets halfway through. The scones are ready when their tops are golden brown and some of the jam or marmalade has bubbled over onto the pan. To keep the scones from sticking to the pan, slide a thin spatula underneath them while they're still warm and move them to a baking rack. The scones are best eaten warm from the oven or later that same day.

Coconut Cookies

Butter for the baking sheets

DRY MIX:

$1^3/4$ cups barley flour

$1/2$ cup coconut flour

$3/4$ teaspoon kosher salt

$1/2$ teaspoon baking soda

$1/2$ teaspoon baking powder

WET MIX:

2 eggs

$1/2$ cup sugar

$1/2$ cup dark brown sugar

$1^1/4$ cups light coconut milk

2 teaspoons pure vanilla extract

6 ounces ($1^1/2$ sticks) unsalted butter, at room temperature

FINISH:

$2^1/2$ cups shredded unsweetened coconut

These pretty, rounded cookies have shreds of crunchy coconut on the outside and a soft, cakey interior. They're made from barley flour and coconut flour only—there isn't any all-purpose flour in the recipe, although you'd never know it from the light crumb. I came upon coconut flour one day in the baking aisle of a natural-food store. The label said that it was ground from whole coconuts. Intrigued, I brought it home to see what it was like. The flour smelled just like a fresh coconut. At first, it was difficult to bake with, as it has a tendency to be gummy. Determined to make a cookie from this flour, I tried over and over until it came out right.

These cookies can go straight from the mixing bowl to the oven, or you can chill the cookies and bake them later—they'll taste the same, but the shapes will be different. They'll be slightly softer and will spread more if baked immediately, and they'll be firmer with a more mounded dome if chilled first.

1. Position two racks in the upper and lower thirds of the oven and preheat to 350°F. Rub two baking sheets lightly with butter.

2. Sift the dry ingredients into a large bowl, pouring back into the bowl any grain or other ingredients that may remain in the sifter, and set aside.

3. Crack the eggs into the bowl of a standing mixer fitted with a whisk. Whisk the eggs on low speed to break them up. Add the sugars, increase the speed to high, and mix until the color of milky coffee, about 3 minutes.

4. Measure out the coconut milk and vanilla and set aside.

5. Add the sifted dry ingredients to the egg mixture. Mix on low speed until combined. Add the butter and mix. Add the coconut milk and vanilla and mix until combined. Add 1 cup of shredded coconut and use a spatula to mix it in by hand. Make sure to scrape down to the bottom of the bowl to mix in any ingredient that may have been left behind.

6. Measure the remaining $1^1/2$ cups of coconut into a shallow bowl. Scoop balls of dough about 3 tablespoons in size and dip the rounded side into the coconut. Gently lift them out of the coconut and place them on the prepared baking sheets, coconut side up, leaving about 2 inches between them.

7. Bake for 16 to 20 minutes, rotating the pan halfway through, until the coconut crust is lightly toasted and the bottoms of the cookies are evenly brown. Use a spatula to transfer the cookies to a baking rack and bake the next round. These cookies are best eaten warm from the oven or later that same day. They'll keep in an airtight container for up to 3 days.

Barley **Crêpes**

Butter for the pan

¾ cup whole milk

½ cup medium-bodied beer

2 tablespoons unsalted
   butter, melted and cooled
   slightly

2 teaspoons unsulphured
   molasses (not blackstrap)

2 eggs

1 cup barley flour

½ teaspoon kosher salt

FINISH:

Apple Butter (see page 198)

When you open up a bag of barley flour, the malty, tangy scent may remind you of a brewery, which makes sense since a lot of beer is made from barley malt. These crêpes accentuate that connection, with a generous pour of dark beer added to the batter for moisture as well as flavor. Use a robust, medium-brown ale rather than a dark malt, which can be overwhelming. A bit of molasses complements the beer's slight bitterness. Slather the crêpes with homemade Apple Butter (see page 198) and have them at the end of a meal for dessert, served with the rest of the beer.

1. In the order listed, measure all the ingredients into a blender jar. Blend the batter until it is smooth and free of clumps. Pour the batter into a bowl or a pitcher. Cover and leave the batter at room temperature for at least 1 hour.

2. Use a spoon to stir the batter together, incorporating any of the liquid that may have separated.

3. Heat an 8-inch cast-iron or nonstick pan over medium high heat until a splash of water sizzles when it hits the pan. Rub the pan with butter and hold it at an angle so the handle is close to your body and tilted up, with the edge across from the handle tilted down toward the flame.

4. Using a 2-ounce ladle or ¼-cup measuring cup, scoop up some batter. Pour the batter just off-center in the pan and quickly swirl it around, aiming for one circular motion that creates a thin, even spread of batter in the pan. Do not add more batter to make up for empty space.

5. Cook the crêpe for about 1 minute, until the batter begins to bubble and the edges begin to brown. Slide a metal spatula along the edge to loosen the crêpe, pinch the edge, and flip the crêpe over in one motion. Cook for 45 seconds longer, or until the crêpe is speckled brown and crisp around the edges.

6. The crêpes are best eaten straight from the pan after being folded in half and then in half again, making frilly-edged triangles.

7. If the crêpes are made in advance, lay them individually on a baking sheet in a 400°F oven for 5 to 6 minutes, or until they are warm and tender. The crêpes can also be warmed individually in a pan. They can also be frozen, with parchment paper layered between each crêpe, wrapped tightly in plastic.

Crêpe Batter

Crêpe batter can be made in advance and chilled for up to one day. Before you griddle the crêpes, bring the batter to room temperature. This may take about two hours—be patient, for it's very important for the success of this recipe. Room-temperature crêpe batter will yield a crêpe that is lighter and thinner than one made with chilled batter.

Barley Porridge

This porridge is like a stovetop rice pudding, and like any good rice pudding, it can be either a breakfast or a dessert. Instead of the more traditional rice, I use barley that's been cooked in a cardamom-infused milk. For more flavor, the barley is first toasted in a bit of butter. Pearled barley isn't technically a whole grain, as the bran has been removed, but it's the form most commonly available in markets. If you can find whole-grain barley groats, try using them—just check to see how the cooking time compares. This is warm and comforting served as it is, but it's truly wonderful when served with Fig Compote (see page 196).

1. To toast the barley, melt the butter in a medium pot. Adjust the flame to medium and add the barley and salt. Toast for about 5 minutes, stirring frequently so that the barley toasts evenly and doesn't burn. The grains need to be toasted until they're about two shades darker than they are raw; keep a few raw grains on the counter next to you as a reference point.
2. Add 1½ cups of water to the toasted barley. Cover the pot, reduce the heat to medium low, and cook the grains at a rapid boil until al dente (or barely tender), about 15 minutes.

3. Add all remaining ingredients, stir, and reduce the heat to low. Cook the barley, uncovered, for 55 to 65 minutes, stirring occasionally, until the grains are tender to the bite and the pudding is creamy around the grains.
4. To serve, spoon the porridge evenly between four bowls. Top each bowl with a quarter of the fig compote, if desired. Serve immediately.

2 tablespoons unsalted butter
¾ cup pearled barley
¼ teaspoon kosher salt
2¾ cups whole milk
¼ cup heavy cream
1 tablespoon sugar
⅛ teaspoon ground cardamom

FINISH:
Fig Compote (see page 196), optional

Maple Pecan **Granola**

Butter for the baking sheets
   or roasting pan

DRY MIX:

2 cups pecan halves

3 cups barley flakes

2 cups natural unsweetened
   shredded coconut

1/2 cup wheat bran

SYRUP:

1 cup good-quality maple
   syrup, preferably organic

2 ounces (1/2 stick) unsalted
   butter, cut into small
   pieces

1 teaspoon kosher salt

FINISH:

1 1/2 cups dried blueberries

Granola is something I eat with my fingers as a snack rather than for breakfast with milk poured on top. Filled with chewy dried blueberries, shreds of coconut, and toasty pecans, this granola I grab by the handful. When working with maple syrup, the challenge is capturing its wonderful flavor without the granola becoming overly sweet. Boiling down the maple syrup does just the trick. The reduced syrup is more intensely flavored and it coats the barley flakes better, giving this granola its shine.

Any rolled flakes that you have on hand will work here—either the familiar rolled oats, or the rolled versions of other whole grains such as spelt, rye, or barley, my favorite, which are now frequently stocked in cereal or baking aisles.

1. Heat the oven to 325°F. Spread the pecans onto a baking sheet and toast for 25 minutes, stirring halfway through, until toasty and light golden-brown. (Remember that they will color more in the oven when the granola bakes.)

2. Butter two rimmed baking sheets or a large roasting pan.

3. Measure the barley flakes, coconut, wheat bran, and toasted pecans into a large bowl and toss them together with your hands. Squeeze half the pecans to break them down into pieces.

4. To make the syrup, measure the maple syrup into a small, heavy-bottomed saucepot. Place it over a medium-high flame for about 7 minutes and reduce the syrup to about 3/4 cup. It's fine if it is slightly more than 3/4 cup, but do not let it go below that amount or the granola will lose its gloss. After measuring, pour the reduced syrup back into the pot and add the butter and salt. Swirl the syrup until the butter melts.

5. As soon as the syrup is done, immediately pour it over the barley mixture, making sure to use a spatula to scrape every last bit out. Use the spatula to coat every flake with syrup. This means going over and over, tossing and scraping the flakes together. Scrape the granola evenly over the prepared baking sheets or roasting pan, spreading it evenly in a single, clumpy layer on each surface.

Note: Baking granola is easiest in a pan with a rim, to contain the many loose ingredients. If your baking sheets have rims, use those; otherwise use a large roasting pan on the center rack of the oven. The granola needs a lot of surface area for even baking, so resist the temptation to bake all of the granola on one baking sheet.

6. Bake for 10 minutes. Remove the sheets from the oven, close the oven door to retain the heat, and scrape the outer edges of the granola toward the center and the center out to the edges. Work gently to maintain the crunchy clumps. Put the top sheet on the bottom rack and the bottom sheet on the top rack to ensure even baking, and repeat the baking and scraping a second and third time, for a total of 30 minutes. I prefer my granola on the darker end of the spectrum; if you don't, you might want to take the granola out after 5 to 6 minutes of the last bake.

7. Take the baking sheets out of the oven and allow the granola to cool thoroughly on the sheets; this allows clumps to form. Once the granola has cooled, sprinkle in the dried blueberries. The granola will keep, stored in an airtight container, for at least 1 week.

Clearly Maple

Trying to find a way around the sweetness in early batches of the Maple Pecan Granola, I searched the aisles of grocery stores looking for ways to boost the maple flavor. I found Clearly Maple by Maple Gold, a jar of amber-colored, intensely flavored syrup that is as thick as honey but made from pure maple syrup. Using this product allowed me to reduce the sweetness in the granola while still retaining the great maple flavor. Since not everyone will have access to this product, I call for a reduction of maple syrup in the recipe. However, if you come across Clearly Maple, usually found in well-stocked grocery stores, you can make the granola recipe as follows:

Substitute the syrup ingredients with:

$1/2$ cup maple syrup
2 ounces butter
3 tablespoons Clearly Maple
1 teaspoon kosher salt

Replace step 4 with this: Measure the ingredients into a small, heavy-bottomed saucepot. Place it over a medium flame, stir once, and cook until the syrup comes to an even boil, about 4 minutes. Continue with step 5.

Bird **Crackers**

These crackers are softer and thicker than most and sprinkled with two kinds of seeds, pale sesame and charcoal-colored poppy seeds. The unusual addition of finely grated cooked egg yolk gives the crackers a remarkably moist crumb. To keep the crackers tender, the dough is rolled out only once and cut into rough squares. These crackers are fantastic with a bit of mild goat cheese or topped with smoked fish.

1. Fill a small saucepan with cold water and gently drop in the eggs. Bring the water to a boil. Once the water boils, turn the heat off and leave uncovered for 18 minutes. Drain the hot water and fill the saucepan, with the eggs still in it, with an ice-water bath.

2. Meanwhile, position racks at the upper and lower thirds of the oven and preheat to 450°F. Butter two baking sheets.

3. Sift the flours, sugar, baking powder, salt, and seeds into a large bowl, pouring back into the bowl any bits of grain or other ingredients that may remain in the sifter, and set aside.

4. Add the softened butter to the dry ingredients and use your hands to rub the mixture until the butter is the size of small peas and grains of rice. Peel the eggs and discard the shells and whites. Using a fine grater or a microplane, grate the yolks into the mixture, and stir. Add the milk and stir until just combined.

5. Scrape the dough onto a well-floured surface, folding it once or twice to bring it together, being careful not to overmix. Roll the dough out $3/16$ inch thick and into a rough square or rectangle— only roll the dough out once for tender crackers. Use a pastry cutter or a knife to cut the dough into rough 2 inch by 2 inch squares—keep the rough edge for character. Move the dough to the buttered baking sheets.

6. Whisk the egg into an egg wash (see Sidebar, page 105). Using a pastry brush, lightly brush the egg wash over the squares, twice. Sprinkle the remaining sesame seeds and poppy seeds, and salt to taste, evenly over the squares.

7. Bake for about 10 minutes. The crackers should have pale golden edges and the bottoms will be very lightly colored. These crackers are best eaten the day they're made but can be stored in an airtight container for up to 3 days.

Butter for the baking sheets
2 eggs

DRY MIX:
$1^1/2$ cups barley flour
$1^1/2$ cups all-purpose flour
2 tablespoons powdered sugar
1 tablespoon baking powder
2 teaspoons kosher salt
2 tablespoons sesame seeds,
   natural and untoasted
1 tablespoon poppy seeds

WET MIX:
4 ounces (1 stick) unsalted
   butter, at room temperature
$3/4$ cup whole milk

FINISH:
1 egg for an egg wash
1 tablespoon sesame seeds,
   natural and untoasted
1 tablespoon poppy seeds
Sea or Maldon salt

Hard-Boiled Eggs

Here's a simple technique for boiling an egg that can make the difference between a pure yellow hard-boiled yolk and one that is ringed with an unpleasant layer of greenish gray. Begin by covering eggs with cold water in a pot. Bring the water to a boil, turn the flame off, and set an 18-minute timer. When the timer goes off, drain the eggs, rinse them a few times in cold water, and let them cool in an ice-water bath before peeling them.

buckwheat

If you collect flours like I do, your kitchen sometimes resembles a mill more than a room in a normal house, and your kitchen drawers and cabinets become stocked with jars filled with finely ground powders that all look alike. That isn't the case with buckwheat flour. Its color is so distinctive that it's easy to spot on the counter. It's dark, sometimes almost purple in color, with a sweet smell reminiscent of ripe fruit and a strong, slightly bitter flavor that can take some getting used to.

Traditionally, buckwheat flour is used in Brittany to make galettes, or buckwheat crêpes; in Russia to make blini; and in many countries—Japan, Korea, Italy—to make noodles. Because buckwheat is neither a grain nor a grass but a pseudocereal related to rhubarb, its flour has no gluten and is therefore difficult to bake with unless it is combined with other flours that can lend more structure.

Buckwheat flour is ground from buckwheat groats, also called kasha, which are interesting to cook with in their own right. The groats are hard little kernels, almost triangular in shape. The name "buckwheat" comes from the Middle Dutch for "beech-wheat," as the groats resemble beech-tree nuts—and they have a great texture when cooked correctly. (Don't overcook kasha; al dente it's great, but as mush it's not.)

In the right recipe, buckwheat can be astonishing, lending a rich color and an almost mineral flavor to cookies or scones. In baked goods that don't require gluten, like the Poppy Seed Wafers in this chapter, buckwheat can stand alone. In recipes that need more rise, adding all-purpose flour, in equal or perhaps slightly greater proportion, to the buckwheat gives a muffin or pancake the lift it needs while allowing the flavor of the buckwheat to come through.

It's no coincidence that buckwheat pairs extremely well with fall fruits, because of its assertive, almost winey flavor. In this chapter, pears—sweet, juicy, with a floral taste—add a fantastic dimension to a pancake batter. Persimmons and dark chocolate add sweetness and depth to a batch of muffins.

If, at first, the buckwheat flour is too strong for you use a greater proportion of white flour until you are used to the flavor and can use the amount the recipe calls for.

Pear and **Buckwheat** Pancakes

Fragrant ripe pears and rich honey butter are a great match for the dark, earthy flavors of buckwheat flour in these pancakes—imagine a plate of traditional blini but bigger, heartier, and laden with fruit. Choose a honey with a sweet, mild flavor, such as acacia or orange-blossom. And make sure that your pears are juicy and ripe, but not so soft that they fall apart when you grate them. If you don't have whole-grain pastry flour, use all-purpose flour instead. The pancakes won't have quite the pillowy texture they would with pastry flour, but they'll have the same delicious flavor.

1. Sift the dry ingredients into a large mixing bowl, pouring back into the bowl any bits of grains or other ingredients that may remain in the sifter.

2. Whisk the melted butter, milk, and egg until thoroughly combined.

3. Peel the pears. Using the large holes on a box grater, grate the whole peeled pears into the milk mixture; the pear juice should fall into the milk along with the grated pears.

4. Using a spatula, add the wet ingredients to the dry ingredients and gently combine. For tender pancakes, it is important that you use a light hand as you gently fold the batter with the spatula. The batter should be slightly thick, with small pieces of pears flecked throughout.

5. Although the batter is best if used immediately, it can sit for about an hour on the counter or overnight in the refrigerator. When you return to the batter it will be very thick and should be thinned, 1 tablespoon at a time, with milk—take great care to not overmix.

6. Meanwhile, melt the butter and honey together in a small saucepan and cook until boiling, emulsified, and slightly thickened, 2 to 3 minutes. Pour the honey butter into a serving pitcher and set it in a warm place near the stove.

7. Heat a 10-inch cast-iron pan or griddle over medium heat until water sizzles when splashed onto the pan. Rub the pan generously with butter; this is the key to crisp, buttery edges, my favorite part of any pancake. Working quickly, dollop 1/4-cup mounds of batter onto the pan, 2 or 3 at a time. Once bubbles have begun to form on the top side of the pancake, flip it over and cook until the bottom is dark golden-brown, about 5 minutes total.

8. Wipe the pan with a cloth before griddling the next batch. Rub the pan with butter and continue with the rest of the batter. If the pan is too hot or not hot enough, adjust the flame accordingly to keep results consistent.

9. Serve the pancakes hot, straight from the skillet, with the pitcher of honey butter, encouraging your guests to pour liberally.

Butter for the pan

DRY MIX:

1 cup buckwheat flour

1 cup whole-grain pastry flour

3 tablespoons sugar

2 teaspoons baking powder

3/4 teaspoon kosher salt

WET MIX:

2 tablespoons unsalted butter, melted and cooled slightly

1 1/4 cups whole milk

1 egg

2 medium pears, ripe but firm

FINISH:

4 ounces (1 stick) unsalted butter

1/2 cup honey

Figgy Buckwheat **Scones**

Parchment for the baking
   sheets

DRY MIX:

1 cup buckwheat flour

$1^{1}/_{4}$ cups all-purpose flour

$^{1}/_{2}$ cup sugar

2 teaspoons baking powder

$^{1}/_{2}$ teaspoon kosher salt

WET MIX:

4 ounces (1 stick) cold
   unsalted butter, cut into
   $^{1}/_{4}$-inch pieces

$1^{1}/_{4}$ cups heavy cream

1 cup Fig Butter (see page 199)

I was inspired to create a scone with buckwheat and figs when I realized how similar they are. Both are ripe and jammy, almost winey. Imagine a sophisticated Fig Newton but less sweet. Although this scone recipe may seem a bit more time-consuming than others, remember that the Fig Butter can be made ahead of time.

1. Sift the dry ingredients into a large bowl, pouring back into the bowl any bits of grain or other ingredients that may remain in the sifter.

2. Add the butter to the dry mixture. Rub the butter between your fingers, breaking it into smaller bits. Continue rubbing until the butter is coarsely ground and feels like grains of rice. The faster you do this, the more the butter will stay solid, which is important for the success of the recipe.

3. Add the cream and gently mix it into the flour with a spatula until the dough is just combined.

4. Use a pastry scraper or a spatula to transfer the dough onto a well-floured surface. It will be sticky, so flour your hands and pat the dough into a rectangle. Grab a rolling pin and roll the dough into a rectangle that is 8 inches wide, 16 inches long, and $^{3}/_{4}$ inch thick. If at any time the dough rolls off in a different direction, use your hands to square the corners and pat it back into shape. As you're rolling, periodically run a pastry scraper or spatula underneath to loosen the dough, flour the surface, and continue rolling. This keeps the dough from sticking. Flour the top of the dough if the rolling pin is sticking.

5. Spread the fig butter over the dough. Roll the long edge of the dough up, patting the dough as you roll so that it forms a neat log 16 inches long. Roll the finished log so that the seam is on the bottom and the weight of the roll seals the edge.

6. Use a sharp knife to slice the log in half. Put the halves on a baking sheet or plate, cover loosely with plastic wrap, and chill in the refrigerator for 30 minutes. (The dough can be kept, covered, in the refrigerator for 2 days.) While the dough is chilling, preheat the oven to 350°F. Line two baking sheets with parchment paper.

7. After 30 minutes, take both logs out of the refrigerator and cut each half into 6 equal pieces about $1^{1}/_{4}$ inches wide. Place each scone flat, with the spiral of the fig butter facing up, on a baking sheet, 6 to a sheet. Give the scones a squeeze to shape them into rounds.

8. Bake for 38 to 42 minutes, rotating the sheets halfway through. The scones are ready to come out when their undersides are golden brown. They are best eaten warm from the oven or later that same day.

Chocolate Persimmon **Muffins**

Butter for the tins

DRY MIX:

1 cup buckwheat flour

$1^1/_2$ cups all-purpose flour

$1/_4$ cup plus 2 tablespoons unsweetened natural cocoa powder

2 teaspoons baking powder

1 teaspoon kosher salt

$1/_2$ teaspoon baking soda

WET MIX:

3 ounces ($3/_4$ stick) cold unsalted butter, cut into $1/_2$ inch pieces

$1/_4$ cup dark brown sugar

$1/_4$ cup sugar

2 eggs

$1/_2$ cup plain yogurt

2 cups Hachiya persimmon pulp, from 2 large or 4 small ripe persimmons

4 ounces bittersweet chocolate, 50 to 60 percent cacao, cut into roughly $1/_4$-inch pieces

These muffins are rich and dark, laced with chunks of melted chocolate and orange flecks of caramelized persimmon; cocoa powder and buckwheat flour are the basis of the muffin's crumb. The persimmon, ripe and jammy, also lends moisture, sweetness, and a glorious color.

The inside of a ripe persimmon is as soft as a purée, eliminating the need to do anything more to the pulp than scoop it out. Use a spoon to scoop the pulp, being careful not to break up the few gelatinous wedges in the center of the fruit.

1. Preheat the oven to 350°F. Rub muffin tins with a $1/_3$-cup capacity with butter. Sift the dry ingredients into a large bowl, pouring back into the bowl any bits of grain or other ingredients that may remain in the sifter.

2. Add the butter and the sugars to the bowl of a standing mixer. Attach the paddle, mix on low speed until the ingredients are combined, then turn to high speed and cream until the butter and sugars are light and creamy, about 3 minutes. Using a spatula, scrape down the sides and the bottom of the bowl. Add the eggs and mix on medium speed for about 1 minute, until thoroughly combined. Add the yogurt and mix until combined. Again, scrape down the sides of the bowl.

3. Add the dry ingredients to the bowl and mix on low speed until combined. Remove the bowl from the mixer, add the persimmon pulp and the chopped chocolate, and fold them gently into the batter by hand. Scrape down the sides and the bottom of the bowl to evenly combine the ingredients.

4. Scoop the batter into 8 muffin cups, using a spoon or an ice cream scoop. The batter should be slightly mounded above the edge. There will be a few gelatinous pieces of persimmon in the batter; if you can, take them from the batter and drape or tuck them into the tops of the muffins for a pretty finish.

5. Bake for 33 to 37 minutes, rotating the pans halfway through. As the muffins are dark, it is hard to tell when they are ready to come out. Test the muffin like you would a cake, pressing into its top to see how much give there is; it should spring back lightly. Take the tins out of the oven, twist each muffin out, and place it on its side in the cup to cool. This ensures that the muffin stays crusty instead of getting soggy. These muffins are best eaten warm from the oven or later that same day. They can also be kept in an airtight container for up to 2 days, or frozen and reheated.

Note: To encourage even baking and to allow each muffin enough room to have an individual dome top, fill alternate cups in a 24-cup tin, or use two 12-cup tins.

Kasha **Pudding**

Kasha, the kernel of the buckwheat grain, has a slightly waxy, al dente texture unlike any other grain. This pudding is scented with nutmeg and vanilla and is quite loose and creamy when it's pulled from the oven. If you prefer your pudding thicker, leave it in the oven for a few minutes longer than the recipe suggests, but remember that it will thicken as it cools. Top each bowl of pudding with ripe fruit, as this really brings out the flavor of the vanilla bean.

1. Preheat the oven to 400°F. Add the kasha, $3/4$ cup water, butter, and salt to a 2-quart baking dish. If the dish has a lid, put it on; otherwise, cover the dish securely with aluminum foil.
2. Bake for 20 minutes, or until the kasha is al dente and the water has been absorbed.
3. Meanwhile, in a large bowl, stir together the milk, cream, brown sugar, cinnamon sticks, nutmeg, and vanilla bean, adding both the scraped vanilla beans and the pod.
4. After the kasha has had its initial cooking, add the milk mixture to the kasha, stir, replace the lid or foil, and return the dish to the oven to bake for 30 more minutes. After 30 minutes, stir the kasha (it will still be quite thin at this point) and bake the dish, covered, for 15 minutes more. The pudding is done when the kasha is tender and the milk has barely thickened. Don't worry if the pudding seems quite loose, as it will thicken as it cools. If you prefer your pudding thicker, remove the lid after 45 minutes and bake 5 minutes more, uncovered.
5. Let the pudding cool for about 15 minutes before serving. Spoon it into 8 bowls and top with seasonal fruit, if desired.

$3/4$ cup kasha (buckwheat groats)
1 tablespoon unsalted butter
$1/2$ teaspoon kosher salt

$2^1/2$ cups whole milk
1 cup heavy cream
$1/4$ cup dark brown sugar
2 cinnamon sticks
1 teaspoon freshly grated nutmeg
1 vanilla bean, split and scraped

FINISH:
Seasonal fruit for topping, optional

Poppy Seed **Wafers**

Parchment for the baking
  sheets

WET MIX:
1/4 cup plus 2 tablespoons
  heavy cream
2 egg yolks

DRY MIX:
1 1/2 cups buckwheat flour
1 cup all-purpose flour
1 cup sugar
1 1/2 teaspoons kosher salt

6 ounces (1 1/2 sticks) unsalted
  butter, at room temperature

FINISH:
2 tablespoons sugar
2 tablespoons poppy seeds
Egg whites from egg yolks
  above

These crisp cookies are delicious in the middle of the afternoon when you want a little something sweet or served with a cup of tea. The thin, elegant wafers have a fine sandiness and a slight acidic earthiness that comes from the buckwheat flour. My husband, Thomas, had the idea to roll the dough in poppy seeds to add a little texture to the delicate cookie. The logs of dough can be formed and chilled or frozen ahead of time so that they're ready when you need them. Using parchment makes it easier to lift these cookies from the baking sheet.

1. Measure the cream and egg yolks into a small bowl—no need to whisk—and set aside.

2. Sift the dry ingredients into a large bowl, pouring back into the bowl any bits of grain or other ingredients that may remain in the sifter. Add the softened butter to the dry ingredients. With your hands, squeeze the butter into the flour. After the butter is mostly blended in, add the cream and egg yolks. Continue squeezing the mixture until a crumbly dough forms. Scrape the dough onto a well-floured surface and, using the palm of your hand, smear the dough to fully incorporate all the ingredients.

3. Divide the dough in half. Roll each piece of dough into a log that is 8 inches long and 1 3/4 inches wide, flouring the dough and work surface as needed. Chill the logs for 2 hours. If the dough is more lopsided than round, you can gently roll the dough again after 15 minutes or so.

4. In a small bowl, stir together the sugar and poppy seeds and pour onto a plate. Brush one log very lightly with the egg whites. (I find it easiest to stand the log on one end as I brush it.) Roll the log in the poppy seed mixture until it is entirely covered. Repeat this process with the remaining log and chill while the oven is heating up, or wrapped in plastic for up to 5 days.

5. Place two racks in the upper and lower thirds of the oven and preheat to 350°F. Line two baking sheets with parchment. Slice the logs into 1/8-inch wafers. Arrange the wafers on the baking sheets.

6. Bake for 15 to 17 minutes, rotating the sheets halfway through. The wafers should be dark golden-brown, with a darker ring around the edge, and smell quite nutty. Cool the cookies on a rack and repeat with the remaining wafers.

7. These wafers are best eaten the day that they're made, but they'll keep in an airtight container for up to 1 week.

Note: Rolling these logs of dough can be a bit tricky at first. When forming a log, squeeze the dough together to lengthen it, trying not to roll the dough over itself, which can create a pocket in the center. Work quickly to avoid softening the dough, which makes it more difficult to roll. The coating of poppy seeds and sugar is added once the logs have had some time to chill, as it makes it easier to apply and gives the wafers a prettier edge.

corn

Corn is a lot more than just fresh kernels on a cob. Dried and ground to lesser or greater degrees, corn can be used for masa, polenta, cornbread, tortillas, or grits. Countless dishes in Mexican cuisine are made from corn, from drinks like *champurrado* to the spicy soup *pozole*, which is made with hominy.

The New World was built on corn, and these days corn products permeate much of the food in America: high fructose corn syrup, corn starch and corn oil, even much of the fuel that drives these products to their destinations. With so many corn products on the market, I was shocked to find corn flour in the whole-grain section of my local grocery store. How had that very basic form—flour—escaped my attention? Ground to a fine powder, corn flour is warm and dusty, surprisingly bitter but with sweet undertones. It can be bright yellow or more muted, but either way it's like sunlight in a bag.

And while I love cornmeal of every grade, whether ground as coarse as polenta or as fine as sand, corn flour was a welcome find. Instead of trying to work around the grittiness of cornmeal, I sifted corn flour into doughs and muffins and discovered that I could get the full flavor and gorgeous color of corn without the rough bite. Now I could control the texture, starting with soft corn flour and building out, adding as much or as little of the coarser grains as I wanted to the recipe.

To compensate for the absence of gluten in corn flour, I combine it with all-purpose flour, or with whole-grain pastry flour for an even softer texture. With the right proportions, baked goods made with corn flour are tender and have good structure, with a subtle flavor that can go either sweet or savory.

Corn accentuates the flavors of Gruyère, highlights the green onions, and provides a contrast for the fruity spice of cumin in the Corn and Gruyère Muffins in this chapter. Corn is also impressive when paired with fruit, as its faintly musky flavor complements the sweetness. In the Rhubarb Tarts, the assertive tanginess and rich magenta color of rhubarb also pairs particularly well with corn in a pretty little tart made with a corn-flour crust.

Honey Polenta **Cornbread**

Butter for the pan

1 cup coarse polenta grains,
   or cornmeal
1/4 teaspoon kosher salt

DRY MIX:

1 1/2 cups graham flour
1 cup millet flour
1 cup all-purpose flour
1/4 cup sugar
2 teaspoons baking powder
1 teaspoon baking soda
2 teaspoons kosher salt

WET MIX:

4 ounces (1 stick) unsalted
   butter
1 cup whole milk
1/4 cup honey
1/4 cup unsulphured (not
   blackstrap) molasses
3 eggs

GLAZE:

2 tablespoons (1/4 stick)
   unsalted butter
1/4 cup honey
1/4 teaspoon kosher salt

One day, faced with a large amount of cooked polenta, I thought to stir some into a batch of cornbread for dinner. It was the best pan of cornbread I'd ever made, moist, with a nice grainy chew. So this recipe calls for par-cooked polenta, which means an extra step in your kitchen, but you'll find it's well worth the effort. I tested this recipe with purchased, precooked polenta, just to see if I could eliminate a step, but it wasn't successful. So just make your own, and eat any extra with some wilted greens and a bit of grated cheese.

This cornbread is delicious—wholesome with a fine crumb and a swirl of honey butter throughout. When the cornbread is hot from the oven even more honey butter is brushed over the top as a glaze, which gives the crust its sheen and an extra-sweet bite.

1. Position a rack in the middle of the oven and preheat to 350°F. Butter a 2 1/2 quart baking dish.

2. Make the polenta: In a medium pot, bring 3 cups of water and the salt to a boil. Sprinkle in the polenta grains, stirring constantly to prevent clumping. Turn the heat to low. Continue cooking, stirring occasionally, until the polenta is thick and creamy, about 10 to 15 minutes.

3. To make the glaze, melt the butter, honey, and salt in a small saucepan. Whisk the glaze until smooth, and set aside.

4. Sift the dry ingredients into a large bowl, pouring back into the bowl any bits of flour or other ingredients that may remain in the sifter, and set aside.

5. As soon as the polenta is done, measure 1 cup of it into a medium bowl, add the butter, and stir until the butter is melted and the polenta is smooth. Add the milk, honey, molasses, and eggs to the polenta bowl and whisk until thoroughly combined.

6. Using a spatula, mix the wet ingredients into the dry ingredients, folding the batter and mixing until just combined. Pour half of the batter into the pan and smooth, drizzle a third of the honey butter over the batter, scrape the rest of the batter over the glaze, spread the batter evenly and smooth the top. Drizzle more of the honey butter over the top, reserving the last third to brush over the finished cornbread.

7. Bake for about 50 minutes, or until the top is golden brown, the edges have pulled slightly from the side of the pan and a skewer inserted into the center of the bread comes out clean.

8. While the cornbread is hot, brush the last of the glaze over the top crust. The cake can be eaten warm or cool from the pan, or it can be cooled, wrapped tightly in plastic, and kept for up to 2 days.

Corn and Gruyère Muffins

These savory muffins are a great accompaniment to steaming pots of soups and stews, and they go particularly well with chili. If you don't have whole-grain pastry flour, substitute all-purpose flour, though the muffins won't be quite as tender. These muffins are best eaten warm from the oven. This doesn't mean that you have to make them in the hectic rush before dinnertime, however—the batter can be made ahead and refrigerated, and the muffins can be baked when you're ready.

1. Preheat the oven to 350°F. Rub muffin tins with a ⅓-cup capacity with butter.

2. Trim and rinse the green onions. Slice the entire onion from end to end into thin circles. Toast the cumin in a small sauté pan over medium heat until they pop and turn golden brown, about 2 minutes. Melt the butter in the same sauté pan, with the cumin still in it, over medium heat. This infuses the butter with cumin. Add the onion, season with salt and pepper, and sauté until the onions are tender and begin to wilt, about 2 minutes. Scrape the onions onto a plate to cool slightly.

3. Sift the dry ingredients into a large bowl, pouring back into the bowl any bits of grain or other ingredients that may remain in the sifter. Add the grated cheese and cooled onion-and-cumin mixture, stirring to combine.

4. In a small bowl, whisk together the sour cream, eggs, and melted butter. Using a spatula, add the wet ingredients to the dry ingredients and gently combine.

5. Scoop the batter into 10 muffin cups, using a spoon or an ice cream scoop. The batter should be slightly mounded above the edge.

6. Bake for 32 to 36 minutes (or a few minutes longer if the batter was chilled first), rotating the pans halfway through. The muffins are ready to come out when their bottoms are golden brown (twist a muffin out of the pan to check). Take the tins out of the oven, twist each muffin out, and place it on its side in the cup to cool. This ensures that the muffin stays crusty instead of getting soggy. These muffins are best eaten warm from the oven. They can also be kept in an airtight container for up to 2 days, or frozen and reheated.

Butter for the tins

1½ cups sliced green onions
2 teaspoons cumin seed
1 tablespoon unsalted butter
Salt and pepper to taste
2 cups grated Gruyère
   cheese, about ⅓ pound

DRY MIX:

1 cup corn flour
1 cup whole-grain pastry
   flour
¼ cup dark brown sugar
2 teaspoons baking powder
½ teaspoon baking soda
1 teaspoon kosher salt

WET MIX:

1½ cups sour cream
2 eggs
2 ounces (½ stick) unsalted
   butter, melted and cooled
   slightly

Note: To encourage even baking and to allow each muffin enough room to have an individual dome top, fill alternate cups in a 24-cup tin, or use two 12-cup tins.

Rhubarb Tarts

MAKES 10 INDIVIDUAL TARTS

Parchment for the baking sheets

DRY MIX:

1 cup corn flour

1 cup all-purpose flour

1/2 cup fine cornmeal

1/4 cup plus 2 tablespoons sugar

1 teaspoon kosher salt

WET MIX:

4 ounces (1 stick) cold unsalted butter, cut into 1/2-inch pieces

1/4 cup plus 2 tablespoons heavy cream

2 egg yolks

1 batch Rhubarb Hibiscus Compote (see page 194)

Free-form tarts are my favorite way to showcase ripe fruit—they're delicious, easy and beautiful without being precious. Here, corn flour and rhubarb are paired for both their assertive flavor and their stunning color. You can also press the dough into a fluted tart shell for a larger, more formal dessert. Or, just make the dough (without the compote) and roll into simple cookies.

1. To make the dough, sift the dry ingredients into the bowl of a standing mixer, pouring back into the bowl any bits of grain or other ingredients that may remain in the sifter.
2. Attach the bowl and the paddle to the standing mixer. Add the butter, turn the mixer speed to low (so the flour doesn't go flying out of the bowl) and mix to break up the butter. Increase the speed to medium and mix until the butter is as coarse as cornmeal. Add the heavy cream and the egg yolks and mix until combined. The dough will appear crumbly, but when squeezed between your fingers it will become one mass. This dough is best shaped right after making, as it hardens when refrigerated. If the dough is chilled first, let it come to room temperature before shaping.
3. To shape the tarts, divide the dough into 10 equal pieces. Lightly flour a work surface. Grab one piece of dough and, using the heel of your hand, flatten the dough into a rough circle. Continue flattening until the circle is approximately 5 inches in diameter and of even thickness. If at any time the dough is sticking, flour the work surface and the dough. For an elegant finish, gently flatten the outer edge in a downward fashion, making it thinner than the rest of the dough.
4. Spoon 1/4 cup of rhubarb compote into the center of the dough. Fold the edge of the dough toward the compote and up, to create a ruffled edge. Continue until an irregularly shaped ruffling happens. (Keep in mind that this is a rustic, handmade tart, so it shouldn't look like a machine made it.)
5. Slide a bench scraper or metal spatula underneath the tart and transfer it to a plate or baking sheet. Continue with the remaining dough. Slide the shaped tarts into the freezer to rest and harden for at least 1 hour, or up to 2 weeks if wrapped tightly in plastic.
6. Preheat the oven to 375°F. Line two baking sheets with parchment. Transfer the tarts onto the baking sheets.
7. Bake for about 35 minutes, or until the edges of the tarts are brown and the rhubarb is bubbling and thick.
8. The tarts can be eaten warm or at room temperature. They can also be wrapped tightly in plastic and kept for up to 2 days.

Carrot and **Corn-Flour** Waffles

MAKES 10

2 ounces (½ stick) butter, melted, for the waffle iron

DRY MIX:

1½ cups corn flour

1½ cups all-purpose flour

¼ cup plus 2 tablespoons wheat germ

¼ cup dark brown sugar

1 tablespoon baking powder

1 tablespoon ground ginger

1½ teaspoons kosher salt

WET MIX:

1 cup plus 2 tablespoons carrot juice

¾ cup whole milk

3 tablespoons unsalted butter, melted and slightly cooled

Zest and juice of one orange

2 eggs

Sometimes the best cooking inspiration comes from what's in your cupboards. One cold Sunday morning in winter, I wanted to use a handful of corn flour in a batch of waffles for the kids. As I pulled milk, butter, and eggs from the fridge, I noticed a small glass of carrot juice, and on a whim I poured it into the batter. Both the carrots and the corn flour had a sunny sweetness that made them a perfect breakfast match. The juice and zest of an orange brightened the flavor and color of the waffles. When you make this recipe for breakfast, squeeze some extra oranges and serve a pitcher of juice along with the waffles.

1. Turn the waffle iron to its highest setting. Even if you don't usually heat it this high, these waffles come out best when cooked at high heat. Sift the dry ingredients into a large bowl, pouring back into the bowl any bits of grain or other ingredients that may remain in the sifter.

2. In a medium bowl, whisk all the wet ingredients together until thoroughly combined and a creamy orange color. Pour the wet mixture into the dry, using a spatula to get every last bit. With a light hand gently fold the two mixtures together. The batter will be thick and pillowlike, with large pockets of deflated bubbles on the surface.

3. Brush the waffle iron generously with butter; this is the key to a crisp crust. Use a ladle or measuring cup to scoop ½ cup batter onto the spaces of the iron. Promptly close, and listen for the iron to sigh as the batter begins to cook. The smell wafting from the iron starts out like a freshly kneaded loaf of bread, then becomes toasty. Remove the waffle when the indicator light shows that it is done, or when a quick peek shows that it's turned a dark golden-brown, 4 to 6 minutes. Remove the hot waffle with a fork, and repeat with the remaining batter.

4. The waffles should be served hot—right out of the waffle iron—as the buttery flavors and beautiful crunch tend to deteriorate quickly when the waffles cool. Serve with a large knob of unsalted butter and the best maple syrup you can find, or with some Three-Citrus Marmalade (see page 192). Or add a spoonful of Greek yogurt to the plate, use the back of the spoon to make a hollow, and drop a bit of syrup or jam into it.

92   GOOD TO THE GRAIN

Cornmeal Blueberry Cookies

These cookies are gorgeous little domes with a tawny yellow crumb and indigo flecks of dried blueberries. They have a delicate sugar crust and a soft center. The crumb comes from using both finely ground cornmeal and powdery yellow corn flour. Resist the urge to use a coarser cornmeal, as it can give the cookies an unpleasant grittiness. Dried blueberries can vary tremendously, with some barely sweetened and others so sweet that they seem more like candy than dried fruit. Since these cookies depend on granulated sugar for their texture, use dried blueberries that aren't too sweet—taste some first to see if you like the flavor.

Butter for the pans

DRY MIX:

2 cups corn flour

2 cups all-purpose flour

1 cup finely ground cornmeal

1½ teaspoons baking soda

2 teaspoons cream of tartar

2 teaspoons kosher salt

WET MIX:

8 ounces (2 sticks) cold
   unsalted butter,
   cut into ½-inch pieces

2 cups dark brown sugar

2 eggs

¼ cup whole milk

1 cup dried blueberries

FINISH:

½ cup sugar

1. Place two racks in the upper and lower thirds of the oven and preheat to 350°F. Rub two baking sheets with butter.

2. Sift the dry ingredients into a large bowl, pouring back into the bowl any bits of grain or other ingredients that may remain in the sifter, and set aside.

3. Add the butter and the brown sugar to the bowl of a standing mixer fitted with a paddle attachment. Turn the mixer to low speed and mix until the butter and sugar are combined, then increase the mixer speed to medium and cream for 2 minutes. Use a spatula to scrape down the sides and the bottom of the bowl.

4. Add the eggs, one at a time, mixing until each is combined. Add the flour mixture to the bowl and blend on low speed until the flour is barely combined, about 20 seconds. Scrape down the sides and the bottom of the bowl. Add the milk and the blueberries. Slowly mix until the dough is evenly combined.

5. Pour the finishing sugar into a bowl. Scoop mounds of dough, each about 3 tablespoons in size, form them into balls, and set them on a plate. Dip each ball into the sugar, coating it lightly. Arrange the balls on the baking sheets, leaving about 3 inches between them. The balls of dough that don't fit on this round of baking can be dipped in the sugar and chilled.

6. Bake the cookies for 20 to 22 minutes, rotating the sheets halfway through. The cookies will puff up and crack at the tops and are ready to come out when the sugar crust is golden brown and the cracks are still faintly yellow.

7. Repeat with the remaining dough.

8. These cookies are best eaten warm from the oven or later that same day. They'll keep in an airtight container for up to 3 days.

kamut

Kamut (pronounced ka-MOOT) flour is amber in color and has a smooth, buttery flavor with a faint earthiness. Smell a bag of it and you'll find hints of wet straw and bread rising. The flavor is mild, almost sweet, and without the bitterness of many wheat varieties. This mildness, along with its fine texture, gives Kamut flour remarkable versatility and makes it particularly well suited to pastries and baked goods. Kamut flour is especially good in recipes in which butter plays a key role, such as brioche, challah, and sugar cookies, as the rich butter in these recipes brings out the intrinsic buttery flavor of the flour.

Kamut is a grain with an ancient provenance (and a technical name, QK-77, that sounds more like a NASA project than a type of wheat). "Kamut" is actually a brand name for organically grown Khorasan wheat, which, like its close relative durum wheat, traces its ancestry to emmer, a grain that grew wild thousands of years ago in the Fertile Crescent of Mesopotamia.

The modern history of Kamut dates back to 1949, when Earl Deadman, a Montana airman stationed in Portugal, was given 36 kernels of the wheat from a friend who said that they came from an ancient tomb near Dashare, Egypt. (This is possible, although ancient Egyptians probably grew einkorn, the grain that's been found in four-thousand-year-old tombs. Einkorn, according to legend, is the grain Noah carried on the Ark.) Wherever they came from, the grains ended up back in Montana, where the airman's father grew the wheat as a novelty since he couldn't find a commercial market for it. It wasn't until the 1980s and the rise in popularity of natural-foods markets that there was enough interest to grow the grain commercially.

Kamut was given its name by Mack and Bob Quinn, a father-and-son team of Montana organic farmers who knew the airman's family and came into possession of one of the last jars of the seeds in the late 1970s. According to Bob Quinn, they decided on the name "Kamut" after finding a reference in an old hieroglyphic dictionary that cited the word as an ancient Egyptian name for wheat, a word that also meant "soul of the earth." Through their organization, Kamut International, the Quinns now oversee research and production for a growing worldwide market. As it's trademarked, the wheat has never been altered by modern plant-breeding programs.

It's interesting to work with a flour that may have come to this country via an Egyptian tomb (or even Noah's Ark). Even if the story is only legend, it's a reminder that all grains come our way well traveled, with the strangest detours.

Sand Cookies

Butter for the pans

1¾ cups Kamut flour

¾ cup plus 2 tablespoons
powdered sugar

¾ teaspoon kosher salt

6 ounces (1½ sticks)
unsalted butter, at room
temperature

With only four ingredients, this is a quick recipe that highlights the flavor of its few components. Because butter is so central to the flavor of these little cookies, you might want to try using a European-style butter like Plugra, as the rich, creamy flavor of high-quality butter really takes center stage. Formed by rolling the dough into small balls and pressing them lightly with the heel of your hand, the cookies resemble sand dollars when baked—hence the name. They need to be shaped right after the dough is made, as it hardens when chilled.

1. Place two racks in the upper and lower thirds of the oven and preheat to 350°F. Rub two baking sheets with butter.

2. Sift the dry ingredients onto a board or countertop, pouring back any grains or other ingredients that may remain in the sifter. Add the butter to the dry ingredients and use the heel of your hand to rub the butter into it. The dough will be crumbly at first, but it will come together as you work the dough. Once the ingredients are mixed in, knead the dough together a few times.

3. Pinch off pieces of dough 1 generous tablespoon in size. Roll the pieces into balls. Set each ball on the countertop and, using the heel of your hand or your fingers, gently flatten the ball into a shaggy circle about ¼ inch thick and 2 inches across. Repeat with the remaining dough. The shaped cookies can be transferred to a plate or baking sheet, wrapped tightly in plastic and refrigerated for up to 1 week. Or to bake immediately, transfer the cookies to the buttered baking sheets, leaving at least 1 inch between them.

4. Bake for 18 to 20 minutes, rotating the pan halfway through. The cookies should be evenly golden, with darker edges and a dark golden bottom crust. To achieve the signature flavor and sandy texture of these cookies, make sure that they're baked all the way through and darker rather than lighter in color.

5. These cookies are best eaten the day that they're made. They'll keep in an airtight container for up to 3 days.

Pumpkin Pancakes

Butter for the pan

DRY MIX:

1 cup Kamut flour

1 cup all-purpose flour

2 teaspoons baking powder

$3/4$ teaspoon kosher salt

$1/2$ teaspoon baking soda

$1/4$ teaspoon cinnamon

$1/8$ teaspoon allspice

WET MIX:

3 tablespoons unsalted
  butter, melted and cooled
  slightly

$1^1/4$ cups whole milk

1 cup buttermilk

$2/3$ cup pumpkin purée

2 tablespoons honey

1 egg

SPICED SUGAR:

$1/3$ cup sugar

2 teaspoons freshly grated
  nutmeg

$3/4$ teaspoon cinnamon

$1/2$ teaspoon allspice

Puréed pumpkin adds a seasonal flair to these pancakes. I use good-quality canned organic pumpkin, which you can find in grocery stores all year, not just around Thanksgiving. However, if you happen to have any roasted pumpkin or butternut squash left over from dinner, by all means purée it into these pancakes. Here a mixture of sugar, nutmeg, cinnamon, and allspice makes a topping that gives a fantastic crunch to the finished pancakes. Sprinkle the spiced sugar over the pancakes while they're still hot and without any butter, so the sugar doesn't melt.

1. Sift the dry ingredients into a large bowl, pouring back into the bowl any bits of grain and other ingredients that may remain in the sifter, and set aside.

2. In a medium bowl, whisk together the wet ingredients until thoroughly combined.

3. Using a spatula, mix the wet ingredients into the dry ingredients. For tender pancakes, it's important that you use a light hand while gently folding the batter together with the spatula. The batter should be the consistency of lightly whipped cream and have a subtle orange hue.

4. Although the batter is best if used immediately, it can sit for about an hour on the counter or overnight in the refrigerator. When you return to the batter, it will be very thick and should be thinned, 1 tablespoon at a time, with milk—take great care to not overmix. Meanwhile, mix together the spiced sugar and set it aside.

5. Heat a 10-inch cast-iron pan or griddle over a medium heat until water sizzles when splashed onto the pan. Rub the pan generously with butter; this is the key to crisp, buttery edges, my favorite part of any pancake. Working quickly, dollop $1/4$-cup mounds of batter onto the pan, 2 or 3 at a time. Once bubbles have begun to form on the top side of the pancake, flip it over and cook until the bottom is dark golden brown, about 5 minutes total.

6. Wipe the pan with a cloth before griddling the next batch. Rub the pan with butter and continue with the rest of the batter. If the pan is burning too hot or not hot enough, adjust the flame accordingly to keep results consistent.

7. Serve the pancakes hot, straight from the skillet, passing around a bowl of the spiced sugar. Encourage your guests to sprinkle the topping as they please.

Gingerbread **Cake**

This gingerbread is dark and spicy, laced with allspice, aniseed, black pepper, ground coffee, and blackstrap molasses. Freshly grated ginger adds a bright heat, unlike ground ginger, which has a hot, sharp bite. Buy the freshest, youngest ginger you can find, and grate it with a Microplane (a grater with very fine holes). Grate the ginger over the bowl containing the wet ingredients so that you catch any ginger juice that falls from the grater. This is a simple cake that is best served with a dollop of unsweetened, lightly whipped cream.

1. Position a rack in the middle of the oven and preheat to 350°F. Rub a 9-inch round cake pan with butter. In a small sauté pan, toast the aniseed over medium heat, until fragrant and beginning to color. Grind the seeds in a coffee or spice grinder, along with the coffee and black pepper, even if they've been previously ground—this will ensure that everything is evenly ground.

2. Sift the dry ingredients, including the spices, into a large bowl, pouring back into the bowl any bits of grain or other ingredients that may remain in the sifter, and set aside.

3. In a medium bowl, whisk together the wet ingredients until thoroughly combined. Using a spatula, add the wet ingredients to the dry ingredients and gently combine. The batter will be thick, almost mahogany in color, and quite spicy. Using a spatula, scrape the batter into the buttered pan and smooth the top.

4. Bake for 38 to 44 minutes, rotating the pan halfway through. The cake is done when it is dark brown and springs back when lightly touched, or when a skewer inserted in the center comes out clean. The cake can be eaten warm or cool from the pan, or cooled, wrapped tightly in plastic, and kept for up to 2 days.

Butter for the pan

1 teaspoon whole aniseed

1 teaspoon allspice

1 teaspoon freshly ground black pepper

1 teaspoon cinnamon

1 teaspoon finely ground coffee

1 teaspoon freshly grated nutmeg

DRY MIX:

$1^{1}/_{4}$ cups Kamut flour

1 cup all-purpose flour

1 teaspoon baking powder

1 teaspoon baking soda

1 teaspoon kosher salt

WET MIX:

2 ounces ($^{1}/_{2}$ stick) unsalted butter, melted and cooled slightly

1 cup sour cream

$^{3}/_{4}$ cup dark brown sugar

$^{1}/_{2}$ cup unsweetened applesauce

$^{1}/_{4}$ cup unsulphured blackstrap molasses

1 egg

2 tablespoons grated fresh ginger (about a $2^{1}/_{2}$-inch piece)

Cheddar Biscuits

Crusty and cheesy with both cheddar and Parmesan, these biscuits are great in a bread basket with dinner—or just eaten one by one hot from the oven. Buttermilk and crème fraîche give the biscuits a tangy flavor, while a pinch of cayenne and a generous dose of black pepper give them spice. Grating cold butter into the flour is the secret to these biscuits' light and tender crumb. If you've never tried it, it's a quick technique, and a lot easier than breaking up butter with a pastry fork.

1. Position two racks in the upper and lower thirds of the oven and preheat to 350°F. Rub two baking sheets with butter. Sift the dry ingredients into a large bowl, pouring back into the bowl any bits of grain or other ingredients that may remain in the sifter.

2. Using the large holes on a box grater, grate the frozen butter over the dry ingredients. Add the cheddar and the Parmesan and stir until evenly combined.

3. In a small bowl, whisk together the buttermilk and crème fraîche. Add the mixture to the bowl with the dry ingredients, butter and cheeses. Use a spoon or your hands to stir the dough together. As it combines, the dough will have clumps of wet dough next to many smaller, crumblier pieces.

4. Scrape the dough onto a floured work surface and knead it until it roughly comes together, making sure not to overwork the dough, about three kneads. Flour the surface again and use your hands to pat the dough until it's 1 inch thick.

5. Using a 2^1/$_2$-inch round cutter, press straight down through the dough. Twist the cutter and lift it up, moving the biscuit to the buttered baking sheet, leaving a 2-inch space between the biscuits. Continue to cut out circles, gathering the scraps and pressing them together to make more biscuits.

6. Brush the top of each biscuit with buttermilk and sprinkle with a few grinds of black pepper. Bake the biscuits for 35 to 40 minutes, rotating the pan halfway through, until the biscuits are golden brown. The biscuits are best eaten warm from the oven but will keep in an airtight container for 2 days.

Butter for the baking sheets

DRY MIX:

1 cup Kamut flour

^{1}/$_2$ cup whole-wheat flour

2 cups all-purpose flour

2 tablespoons baking powder

1 tablespoon sugar

^{3}/$_4$ teaspoon kosher salt

^{1}/$_2$ teaspoon freshly ground black pepper

^{1}/$_4$ teaspoon cayenne

WET MIX:

4 ounces (1 stick) unsalted butter, frozen

2 cups grated sharp white cheddar, about ^{1}/$_3$ pound

1 cup finely grated Parmesan

1 cup buttermilk

1 cup crème fraîche

FINISH:

2 tablespoons buttermilk

Freshly ground black pepper

Challah

Butter for the bowl

SPONGE:

1 package active dry yeast

1 cup whole milk

1 tablespoon honey

1 cup Kamut flour

1/4 cup millet flour

DOUGH:

2 1/2 cups all-purpose flour,
   plus extra for mixing

1 tablespoon kosher salt

3 eggs

4 ounces (1 stick) unsalted
   butter, at room
   temperature

FINISH:

1 egg for an egg wash

2 tablespoons poppy or
   sesame seeds

Challah, like brioche, is a bread made from dough rich in eggs and butter. Traditionally, the dough is twisted into long ropes to create a braid and then sprinkled with poppy or sesame seeds. I always love reaching into the center of the braid for the soft bread in the middle. This bread uses Kamut flour and millet flour, for both their mildness and their distinctive color. The yellows and golds of the flours, the egg yolks, and the butter produce the challah's traditional tawny color. Challah is best eaten the day it's made, though leftovers make delicious French toast.

1. To make the sponge, pour the yeast into the bowl of a standing mixer. Heat the milk in a small saucepan over low heat to a temperature that is warm to the touch, about 100°F, and pour it over the yeast. Stir together with a spoon to combine. Add the honey, Kamut flour, and millet flour and stir again. Add the all-purpose flour to the top of the sticky dough, then the salt. Do not stir.

2. Let the sponge sit for approximately 30 minutes, until the flour begins to crack and the sponge seeps upward. Meanwhile, set the eggs, in their shells, into a bowl of hot water to bring them to room temperature.

3. After 30 minutes, crack the eggs and add them to the sponge. Put the bowl onto the mixer with the hook attachment and mix on low until the flour is incorporated, scraping down the sides of the bowl with a spatula.

4. Watch the dough to see if it's sticking to the sides. If it is, add additional all-purpose flour, 1 tablespoon at a time—it may take as much as 1/2 cup until the dough is pulling away from the sides of the bowl. Once the dough has formed a cohesive mass and is pulling away from the sides, turn the mixer to medium and set a 5-minute timer. The dough will be moister than many bread doughs and will mostly cohere around the hook, occasionally letting off a tail of dough. Listen for the slapping noises as the dough goes around and around, releasing and incorporating the tail of dough. Halfway through the mixing time, stop the mixer and scrape the dough thoroughly from the hook. Mix the dough for 5 minutes more, making sure to set a timer.

5. After 10 minutes the dough should be a supple, elastic mass. Add the butter

Note: The first step in this dough is a sponge (or, a small amount of the ingredients; usually, yeast, liquid, and flour). A sponge offers the dough the benefits of a longer rise—better flavor and texture—in a shorter amount of time. Basically, it's a head start.

1 tablespoon at a time and mix on medium speed, waiting to add the next piece until the first one is fully incorporated. The dough will come apart and back together again as the butter is incorporated into the dough. Once all the butter is added, the dough should be shiny and soft.

6. For the first rise, scrape the dough into a buttered bowl, cover with a towel or plastic wrap, and leave to rise for 2 hours, or until doubled in size (see Sidebar, page 130). The dough is ready when a floured finger stuck into it leaves an impression. Scrape the dough onto a lightly floured work surface and gently fold the dough into itself and gather it back into a ball.

7. For the second rise, scrape the dough into the bowl, cover with a towel or plastic wrap, and leave to rise for 1 hour, or until doubled in size.

8. For the shaping, dust the dough and the work surface with flour. Scrape the dough out of the bowl and onto the flour. Divide the dough into 3 equal pieces. Lightly flour your hands and roll each piece into a rope about 14 inches long. Pinch the 3 ropes together at one end and begin to braid the dough. The dough is soft and will stretch easily. Take care to lift up each rope as the braid is made and lay it snugly on top of the next piece. The braid should be tight and full. When the braid is finished, pinch the ends of each of the 3 ropes tightly together. Fold under the pinched ends of both sides of the challah.

9. For the third rise, sprinkle a baking sheet with 1 tablespoon of the poppy or sesame seeds. Transfer the braid to the baking sheet, lifting it gently from both ends, with your hands meeting under the dough, taking care to keep it plump rather than letting it stretch out as it is moved. Cover the braid loosely with a towel or plastic wrap and leave to rise for 1 hour.

10. Meanwhile, place a rack in the middle of the oven and preheat to 400°F.

11. Whisk the egg into an egg wash (see Sidebar). Brush the entire surface of the braid with the egg wash and sprinkle with the remaining seeds.

12. Bake for 20 minutes. Reduce the oven temperature to 325°F and bake for an additional 10 minutes. The bread should be a rich, dark golden-brown. Remove the challah from the oven and allow it to cool on a rack before tearing into it. Store any leftover challah as you would a loaf of bread.

Egg Wash

A proper egg wash is one that is creamy yellow and completely mixed together. Use a high-sided medium bowl, one that gives you enough space to thoroughly whisk the egg and not worry about it going over the edges. Crack the egg into the bowl and use a whisk to completely combine the egg. If, when you stop whisking, you can see any clear bits of egg white, whisk some more.

Chocolate **Babka**

Butter and sugar for the pan

1 batch Challah (see page 104),
    made with 8 ounces
    butter instead of 4 ounces

1 cup pecan halves

8 ounces bittersweet
    chocolate, roughly chopped
    into 1/4- and
    1/2-inch pieces

1/2 cup dark brown sugar

1/4 cup sugar

1 teaspoon kosher salt

2 ounces (1/2 stick) unsalted
    butter, at room temperature

This is the ultimate in yeasted coffee cakes. Eastern European in origin, it's made with a yeasted dough enriched with butter and eggs—the same recipe as for challah, but with double the butter, which makes for a very rich cake.

The dough is left to rise overnight in the refrigerator. The next morning, it's rolled out, slathered with more butter, and dusted with sugar, chocolate, and nuts. The adorned dough is rolled into a log, cut into spirals, and fitted, free-form, into a tube or Bundt pan, where it is left to rise. After baking, those spirals give the babka its delicious nooks and crannies filled with melting chocolate and crunchy nuts, which make for an amazing breakfast cake.

1. Make the challah dough and allow it to finish its first rise. Then fold the dough into itself, put it into a buttered bowl, cover, and chill overnight.

2. Preheat the oven to 350°F. Rub a 10-inch pan with butter, then lightly dust it with sugar. Toast the pecans in the pan until golden, about 15 minutes. In a small bowl, stir together the brown sugar, sugar, and salt.

3. Dust a work surface with flour. Remove the challah dough from the refrigerator, flour the top, and scrape the dough onto the work surface. Dust the top of the dough with flour and roll into a rectangle about 10 inches by 16 inches.

4. Rub the softened butter evenly over the surface of the dough. Sprinkle the sugar mix over the butter, then break up the pecans a bit and sprinkle them on top of the sugar. Sprinkle the chocolate last. Starting at the 16-inch length, roll the dough into a tight log. Cut the log into 13 pieces, each about 1 1/4 inches thick.

5. Place the pieces in the pan in a haphazard way, so that as the dough proofs the odd-shaped spaces are filled in. Here is one way: Create the bottom layer by laying 4 circles at the bottom of the pan with the spirals facing up. Set a circle upright in between each of those circles. For the top layer, set 3 circles in areas that will create empty pockets. Slice the last 2 circles in half and fit them into the gaps that remain. Cover the pan with a towel and let the dough rise until doubled in size, about 2 hours.

6. Bake for 45 to 50 minutes. The babka should be a beautiful golden-brown on top and have risen to the top or slightly over the top of the pan. Let it cool slightly, about 15 minutes, before placing a rack on top of the pan and turning the pan upside down to get the babka out of its pan and onto the rack to cool. The babka is best eaten the day it's made. It can be stored, wrapped tightly in plastic, for up to 2 days. When you eat the babka after it's been stored, warm it first.

multigrain

Flours have personalities, distinct flavors, and specific characteristics that deter- mine how they bake and what they taste like. Some of the flours in this book are commonly used and easy to work with. Others are lesser known, have stronger flavors, or require a special touch. Since each flour has strengths and weaknesses, I thought, why not make my own blend?

When I was considering how to introduce whole-grain flours—to my family in the beginning, and then to a wider audience—I thought it would be great to have a multipurpose flour that I could use in virtually any recipe, one that combined all the things I loved about whole grains in one canister.

I first threw some whole-wheat flour into the bowl since it was the most familiar to me. Whole-wheat flour has the strength and rising properties to accomplish pretty much any baking recipe. But the dense texture and heavy crumb it created wasn't what I was looking for. I decided to pair whole-wheat with flours that were lighter and milder. I matched the whole-wheat with equal parts oat and barley flours. Both these flours are sweet, and they balanced the assertive flavor of the whole-wheat perfectly.

To add a bit more complexity, in went smaller portions of millet and rye flours. Millet contains no gluten, so it needs to be added to flours that do, but it brought its lovely yellow color and gentle flavor to the mix. Rye lent structure and also added a malty flavor. When used in large amounts, rye flour can make for a dense and somewhat gummy crumb, so I kept its proportion small.

The combination I settled on is a great shortcut, since I mix up a big batch of Multigrain Flour Mix (see Sidebar) to keep on my kitchen counter. I can easily scoop up a cup or two for a recipe in this chapter, or use the mix in place of another type of flour, like the buckwheat in the Figgy Buckwheat Scones, the spelt in the Carrot Muffins, or the quinoa in the Banana Walnut Cake.

Try out the Multigrain Flour Mix in different recipes and see what the blend can do. It was designed to be versatile. You can also experiment with combinations of your own, keeping in mind that your goal is to create the right balance of flavor and structure.

Multigrain Flour Mix

This is my favorite whole-grain flour mixture, which I call for in the recipes in this chapter. You can make a large amount and keep it, as I do, in a jar on the kitchen counter along with the other flours I use most frequently. If you're only going to use a small amount of this mix, cut the recipe in half.

1 cup whole-wheat flour
1 cup oat flour
1 cup barley flour
1/2 cup millet flour
1/2 cup rye flour

Measure all the flours into a bowl and whisk together.

Beaten **Biscuits**

Butter for the pans

DRY MIX:

1 cup Multigrain Flour Mix
   (see page 109)

1 cup whole-grain pastry
   flour

1 tablespoon baking powder

1 tablespoon sugar

3/4 teaspoon kosher salt

1/2 teaspoon baking soda

WET MIX:

3 ounces (3/4 stick) cold
   unsalted butter, cut into
   1/2-inch pieces

3/4 cup heavy cream

I first tasted beaten biscuits in Kentucky. In the era before baking powder and baking soda, biscuit dough was beaten for long periods of time to give the biscuits lift. Contrary to what I had always thought—that the dough required a light hand to yield a tender biscuit—these biscuits are beaten and folded repeatedly and yet the results are very tender. Here I kept the method, using a bit of chemical leavening with the multigrain flour mix—I didn't quite believe that I would get the lift without it.

These biscuits are small, with a fine, crumbly texture. The homemade multigrain flour mix gives them a pure, sweet, and nutty taste. They are particularly good slathered with Three-Citrus Marmalade (see page 192). The rounds of biscuit dough also make a great topping for a fruit cobbler.

1. Place two racks in the upper and lower thirds of the oven and preheat to 400°F. Rub two baking sheets with butter.

2. Sift the dry ingredients into a large bowl, pouring back into the bowl any bits of grain or other ingredients that may remain in the sifter. Add the butter to the dry mixture. Rub the butter between your fingers, breaking it into smaller and smaller bits until the pieces are the size of grains of rice. The more quickly you do this, the more the butter will stay solid, which is important for the success of the recipe.

3. Add the cream. Working from the outer edge of the flour, draw your hands around the bowl to mix the cream into the flour. Mix until the dough just holds together.

4. Dust a work surface with flour. Use a pastry scraper or a spatula to transfer the dough to the work surface. With a rolling pin, give the dough three good whacks, then fold the dough over and give it three more good whacks. Fold and whack five more times. Flour as needed.

5. Gather the dough into a ball and roll it out to a 3/4-inch thickness. Using a 2-inch round cookie cutter, cut the dough into circles, punching out the circles as close as possible to one another. Gather the excess dough, roll it out again, and punch out more circles. Repeat until all the dough is used, keeping in mind the more times you reroll the dough, the tougher the biscuits will be.

6. Transfer the biscuits to the prepared baking sheets, leaving about 3 inches between them.

7. Bake for 18 to 20 minutes, rotating the pans halfway through. The biscuit tops should be a matte mahogany-brown.

8. Enjoy warm, or even a few hours later. Like all biscuits, they're best eaten the day they're made but will keep in an airtight container for 2 days.

Buttermilk Pancakes

When I crave a stack of pancakes, this is the recipe I reach for. It's a variation on a traditional buttermilk pancake, but with more heft and body than most basic white-flour pancakes. The multigrain flour is mild and subtle, letting the tang of the buttermilk come through, yet giving the pancakes complexity. Serve these with slabs of thick-cut bacon baked with a sprinkling of brown sugar on top.

1. Sift the dry ingredients into a large bowl, pouring back into the bowl any bits of grains or other ingredients that may remain in the sifter, and set aside.

2. In a medium bowl, whisk the wet ingredients until thoroughly combined.

3. Add the wet ingredients to the dry ingredients and, using a spatula, gently mix them together. For tender pancakes, it is important that you use a light hand while gently folding the batter together with the spatula. The batter should be slightly thick, with a holey surface.

4. Although the batter is best if used immediately, it can sit for up to 1 hour on the counter, or overnight in the refrigerator. When you return to the batter it will be very thick and should be thinned, 1 tablespoon at a time, with milk—take great care to not overmix.

5. Heat a 10-inch cast-iron pan or griddle over medium heat until water sizzles when splashed onto the pan. Rub the pan generously with butter; this is the key to crisp, buttery edges, my favorite part of any pancake. Working quickly, dollop 1/4-cup mounds of batter onto the pan, 2 or 3 at a time. Once bubbles have begun to form on the top side of the pancake, flip it over and cook until the bottom is dark golden-brown, about 5 minutes total. Wipe the pan with a cloth before griddling the next batch. Rub the pan with butter and continue with the rest of the batter. If the pan is too hot or not hot enough, adjust the flame accordingly to keep results consistent.

6. Serve the pancakes hot, straight from the skillet, passing around a pitcher of warm syrup and slabs of butter.

Butter for the pan

DRY MIX:

1 cup Multigrain Flour Mix (see page 109)

1 cup whole-wheat flour

2 tablespoons sugar

2 teaspoons baking powder

1 teaspoon baking soda

3/4 teaspoon kosher salt

1/2 teaspoon nutmeg, freshly grated

WET MIX:

2 cups buttermilk

2 tablespoons unsulphured (not blackstrap) molasses

2 eggs

Zest of one orange (about 1 teaspoon)

Five-Grain Cream **Waffles**

2 ounces (½ stick) butter,
   melted, for the waffle iron

DRY MIX:

1 cup Multigrain Flour Mix
   (see page 109)
1 cup whole-grain pastry
   flour
¼ cup sugar
2 teaspoons baking powder
¾ teaspoon baking soda
½ teaspoon kosher salt

WET MIX:

3 eggs
2 cups heavy cream

The multigrain flour mix gives these waffles their complex flavor, tender texture, and nice chewy bite. Two cups of cream make the batter particularly delicate and keep the waffles moist even after they cool. Cook the waffles until they are dark golden-brown, so that the crust has a thin, crisp texture that offsets the fine crumb of the center. Serve these waffles with the best maple syrup you can find and a knob of good butter. For an extra-special treat, try BLiS maple syrup; it's aged in bourbon barrels for a rich, round flavor that is incredible (see Sources, page 200).

1. Turn the waffle iron to its highest setting. Even if you don't usually heat it this high, these waffles come out best when cooked at high heat. Sift the dry ingredients into a bowl, pouring any bits of grain or other ingredients that may remain in the sifter back into the bowl, and set aside.
2. Whisk the cream and eggs together thoroughly. Pour the cream mixture into the dry ingredients, using a spatula to get every last bit. With a light hand gently fold the two mixtures together. The batter will be thick and pillowlike, with large pockets of deflated bubbles on the surface.
3. Brush the waffle iron generously with butter; this is the key to a crisp crust. Use a ladle or a ½-cup measuring cup to scoop batter onto the spaces of the iron. Promptly close, and listen for the iron to sigh as the batter begins to cook. The smell wafting from the iron starts out like a freshly kneaded loaf of bread, then becomes toasty. Remove the waffle when the indicator light shows that it is done, or when a quick peek shows that they've turned a dark golden-brown, 4 to 6 minutes. Remove the hot waffle with a fork, and repeat with the remaining batter.
4. The waffles should be served hot off the griddle.

Popovers

6 eggs

2 1/2 cups milk

1 cup Multigrain Flour Mix
(see page 109)

1 cup all-purpose flour

1 teaspoon kosher salt

4 ounces (1 stick) unsalted
butter, melted and cooled
slightly

Popovers are made from a simple batter that is poured into hot buttered baking tins and baked in a hot oven until they pop up and (sometimes) over, crusty on the outside and custardlike on the inside. They are best eaten immediately, as they deflate as they cool. The batter can sit at room temperature for a few hours before baking. I find that traditional popover pans are not necessary and that muffin tins work just as well. Any size muffin tin will work, but you'll need to adjust the baking time to the size of the cups. This recipe uses a pan with one-third-cup capacity tins (measured with sugar, not water). Just like muffins, popovers bake best with an empty space between them to prevent crowding.

1. Place a rack in the middle of the oven and preheat to 450°F. Place the muffin tins (unbuttered) in the oven to heat up.

2. Measure the eggs, milk, flours, and salt into a bowl or the jar of a blender. Measure half of the melted butter (1/4 cup) over the ingredients in the bowl or blender and pour the other 1/4 cup into a small bowl.

3. Using a hand mixer or the blender, mix the popover batter until combined, about 20 seconds. Remove the muffin tins from the oven and brush every other cup liberally with butter. Working quickly, fill each of the buttered cups three-quarters full with batter.

4. Bake for 15 minutes. Then, rotate the tins and lower the oven temperature to 350°F. Bake for 10 minutes more.

5. Take the tins from the oven, slide a sharp knife around the popovers to remove, and eat immediately. Turn the oven temperature back up to 450°F and repeat with the remaining batter.

Bread and **Butter** Pudding

This is a simple dish created from leftover or stale pieces of bread that are baked in a rich custard. The dessert (or breakfast dish) gets added flavor if you use homemade Baguettes (see page 118), but you can use any purchased baguette or even combine bits of stray bread that you might have on hand. This recipe calls for a larger amount of bread than custard, because I love the way that the bread on the top crisps and browns, contrasting with the soft, sweet interior of what's beneath.

1. Slice the baguette(s) in half lengthwise, then into long strips, and lastly into small pieces about 1 inch in size. You should have about 8 cups of bread. Spread the bread onto a baking sheet. Position a rack in the middle of the oven.

2. Place the baking sheet in the oven and turn the oven to 350°F. (The bread needs a little toast so it doesn't turn into mush while baking in the custard.) Toast for about 12 minutes while the oven is warming up, until the bread is mostly dry and crunchy. Remove from the oven and set aside to cool.

3. Meanwhile, combine the eggs, milk, and cream in a large bowl and mix until thoroughly combined —a whisk works just fine here, but if you have an immersion blender, use that for a quick, smooth blend.

4. Strain the custard into a large bowl. Add the orange zest, juice, sugar, nutmeg, salt, currants, and butter, and stir to combine. Once the bread is cool, add it to the custard. Let the bread and custard soak for 10 minutes, stirring a few times so that the custard is absorbed evenly.

5. Butter a deep 10-inch baking dish or Dutch oven and pour the bread and custard into it. Arrange the bread that sits above the custard in a rustic fashion, spooning the currants that have fallen to the bottom of the bowl across the top of the bread and into the pockets that form on the top.

6. Bake for 1½ hours. After about 1 hour, the tips of the bread will be quite dark, just shy of burning, while the custard will not yet be set. To keep the bread from burning, lay a piece of aluminum foil loosely over the top of the pudding dish. Bake until the pudding has puffed up. Allow it to cool in its pan on top of the stove.

7. The pudding is best served warm or at room temperature the same day it was made. Any leftovers can be wrapped tightly in plastic and refrigerated for 3 days.

Butter for the dish

1 store-bought sourdough, French, or whole-wheat baguette, or ½ recipe (2 small baguettes) of Baguettes (see page 118)

5 eggs

3 cups whole milk

1¼ cups heavy cream

Zest and juice of 2 oranges (no more than ½ cup juice)

¾ cup sugar

1 teaspoon freshly grated nutmeg

¾ teaspoon kosher salt

¼ cup currants

1 tablespoon cold unsalted butter, finely cubed

Iced Oatmeal **Cookies**

These cookies remind me of Mother's® cookies, those crisp oatmeal cookies glazed with icing that come in the signature red-and-purple packages at the store. This recipe makes big cookies with a pale brown-sugar icing that gets its color from a large spoonful of ground cinnamon. If you want thin cookies, bake the dough just after you mix it, before the butter hardens. For thicker, chewier cookies, chill the dough for at least an hour.

1. Place two racks in the upper and lower thirds of the oven and preheat to 350°F. Rub two baking sheets with butter.
2. In a food processor, grind the oats to a coarse meal that still has a few large flakes, about 10 seconds.
3. Sift the dry ingredients into a large bowl, pouring back into the bowl any bits of grains or other ingredients that may remain in the sifter. Add the ground oats to the dry ingredients. In a small bowl, whisk the butter and eggs until thoroughly combined. Using a spatula, add the wet ingredients to the dry ingredients and combine.
4. Scoop balls of dough about 3 tablespoons in size onto the cookie sheets, leaving 3 inches between them, or 6 per sheet—the cookies will spread quite a bit, so be sure not to put them too close together.
5. Bake for 16 to 20 minutes, rotating the sheets halfway through. The cookies are ready to come out when they are evenly brown across the top. Cool the cookies on a rack while you bake the rest of the dough and make the frosting.

6. For the frosting, whisk together the powdered sugar, milk, cinnamon, and salt until smooth and about the consistency of honey. If the frosting is too thick, add a bit more milk. If it's too thin, add a little powdered sugar. Practice your frosting design in the bowl by picking up a whiskful, letting some fall off, and trying to make crazy patterns. The frosting should slip off the whisk slowly, leaving distinct, individual lines.
7. Decorate the cooled cookies on a rack, a sheet of parchment, or a plate. Drizzle the frosting over the cookies one at a time, making irregular lattice designs over the entire tops of the cookies. Let the frosting set for 30 minutes before eating. These cookies are best eaten the day they're made. They'll keep in an airtight container for up to 3 days.

Butter for the baking sheets

DRY MIX:

2 cups rolled oats

2 cups Multigrain Flour Mix (see page 109)

1 tablespoon plus 1 teaspoon baking powder

1 teaspoon baking soda

2 teaspoons kosher salt

1 cup dark brown sugar

1/2 cup sugar

1 teaspoon cinnamon

1 teaspoon freshly grated nutmeg

WET MIX:

8 ounces (2 sticks) unsalted butter, melted and cooled slightly

2 eggs

FROSTING:

2¹/4 cups powdered sugar

5 to 6 tablespoons whole milk

1 tablespoon cinnamon

1/4 teaspoon kosher salt

Baguettes

POOLISH:

3/4 teaspoon active dry yeast

1 1/2 cups Multigrain Flour
Mix (see page 109)

DOUGH:

1 1/2 teaspoons active dry
yeast, or the remaining
part of the package used
for the poolish

1 tablespoon sugar

2 1/2 cups all-purpose flour

1 tablespoon kosher salt

I began my career baking pastries more than bread, so when I first started making baguettes at home I wasn't sure I could get the crunch and chew I wanted from a home oven. But with a lot of practice, and an increasingly hotter oven, I started putting some great loaves of bread on my counters. The time spent on making bread is a large part of what gives it its flavor and texture, but the time can be managed so it doesn't overwhelm your day. This recipe calls for a poolish, a wet, goopy, pre-ferment that is started the night before using small amounts of the same ingredients that will be used in the final dough. This way, when you wake up in the morning you're just a few hours away from delicious homemade baguettes.

1. To make the poolish, measure the yeast into the bowl of a standing mixer. Heat 1 cup of water in a small saucepan over low heat to a temperature that is warm to the touch, about 100°F, and pour it over the yeast. Stir to combine. Add the multigrain flour and stir again. The mixture should be loose, the consistency of yogurt. If it isn't, add either flour or water to adjust it. Cover the bowl with a towel or plastic wrap and let it rise overnight.

2. The next morning, measure the remaining yeast into a small bowl. Heat 3/4 cup of water in a small saucepan over low heat to a temperature that is warm to the touch, about 100°F, and pour it over the yeast. Add this yeast mixture, the sugar, the all-purpose flour, and the salt to the poolish.

3. Mix on low speed until the flour is incorporated, then increase the mixer speed to medium. Watch carefully as the dough begins to form. At first the mass is wet and sticks to the sides of the bowl. Mix for 1 minute to give the flour time to absorb the water before adding flour, 1 tablespoon at a time, until the dough begins to pull away from the sides of the bowl—you should only need 1 or 2 tablespoons. Continue to mix on low speed for 10 minutes; the dough should now be one supple, elastic mass.

4. For the first rise, scrape the dough into an oiled bowl, cover with a towel or plastic wrap, and let rise for 30 minutes. Then, gently pour the dough from the bowl onto a lightly floured surface, allowing it to drop from its own weight.

5. For the second rise, gently fold the dough into thirds (as you would a business letter), put it back into the bowl, cover, and allow to rise for 30 minutes more.

6. For the third rise, again pour the dough onto a lightly floured surface and repeat the process for the second rise. Meanwhile, arrange two racks at the upper and lower thirds of the oven. Place a shallow metal pan on the floor of the oven and preheat to 500°F.

7. To shape the dough, again pour it onto a floured surface, letting it drop from its own weight. Cut the dough into quarters, leaving some space between the quarters. Cover with a towel or plastic wrap and let rest for 30 minutes. Sprinkle flour on two baking sheets.

8. After 30 minutes, take one of the pieces of dough and, with floured hands, fold it in thirds lengthwise (as you would a business letter). Keep drawing up the outer edges of the dough, pinching them at the top, until you have a long torpedo shape, 10 to 12 inches long and approximately 2 inches wide. Roll the ends between the surface and your hands so that they form little tails, and lay the baguette lengthwise on one of the trays. Repeat with the remaining 3 pieces of dough, placing 2 baguettes on each baking sheet. Loosely cover the baguettes with a towel or plastic wrap and allow to rest for 30 minutes.

9. Dust the tops of the baguettes by spooning a little flour into a fine sieve and shaking it over the dough. Don't put too much on; it shouldn't be so thick that it cakes while baking. Slash the tops of the baguettes, deeply, with a very sharp knife (or, ideally, a razor blade). Make 3 or 4 long, diagonal slices, very quickly and with a sure hand so the dough doesn't catch and tear. Immediately slide the trays into the oven. Very carefully, pour 1 cup of water into the pan at the bottom of the oven and quickly shut the oven door. The steam from the water helps give the baguettes a nice crust. Resist the urge to open the oven door, which will let the heat and the steam out of the oven.

10. Bake for about 20 minutes, until the baguettes have a dark golden-brown crust and the little tails are just shy of burning.

11. Allow the baguettes to cool on a baking rack, preferably for a few hours, so that the flavor can develop and the crumb doesn't collapse when you cut into it. The baguettes are best eaten the day they are made.

Spice **Muffins**

Butter for the tins

NUT TOPPING:

1 cup walnuts, halves or
pieces
1/4 cup unsulphured (not
blackstrap) molasses
1 tablespoon sugar
Pinch of kosher salt

DRY MIX:

1 1/2 cups Multigrain Flour
Mix (see page 109)
1 cup all-purpose flour
1/4 cup sugar
1 tablespoon baking powder
1/2 teaspoon baking soda
1 teaspoon kosher salt
1 tablespoon cinnamon
2 teaspoons ginger
1 teaspoon allspice
1/8 teaspoon cloves

4 ounces (1 stick) unsalted
butter, softened to room
temperature

WET MIX:

1/2 cup whole milk
1/2 cup unsweetened
applesauce
1/2 cup unsulphured (not
blackstrap) molasses
2 eggs

A blend of whole-grain flavors and warm spices are the basis of this muffin. The nut topping, made with molasses and walnuts, is fashioned after the wet walnut topping of the old soda fountain days. Blending softened butter into the dry ingredients and then mixing the batter for a relatively long time gives these muffins their fine, tender crumb. Because they are quite soft, the muffins can be tricky to get out of the pan—using paper liners in the cups will solve this problem.

1. Preheat the oven to 350°F. Toast the walnuts until golden, about 15 minutes.
2. Lightly butter the top of the muffin tins, then line the cups with muffin papers. In a medium bowl, stir together the molasses, sugar, and salt. When the nuts are cool, chop them coarsely, stir them into the molasses mixture, and set aside.
3. Sift the dry ingredients into the bowl of a standing mixer, pouring back into the bowl any bits of grain or other ingredients that may remain in the sifter.
4. Add the softened butter to the dry ingredients. Attach the bowl and the paddle to the standing mixer and mix on medium-low speed until the mixture is as coarse as cornmeal, about 1 minute.
5. In a medium bowl, whisk together the wet ingredients until thoroughly combined. Scrape the wet ingredients into the mixing bowl and mix on low speed until combined. Increase the speed to high and mix for 1 minute. Remove the bowl from the mixer and scrape down the sides and the bottom of the bowl.
6. Scoop the batter into 12 muffin cups, using a spoon or an ice cream scoop. The batter should be about even with the tops. Stir the walnut topping to evenly coat the nuts with the molasses. Top the center of each muffin with a spoonful of the nut topping and press the nuts into the batter slightly.
7. Bake for 24 to 26 minutes, rotating the tins halfway through. The muffins are ready to come out when their tops are dark brown and the nuts are toasty and caramelized. Take the pan out of the oven and allow to cool slightly, as the molasses topping is still extremely hot.
8. When the muffins are still slightly warm, twist each muffin out and place it on a baking rack to cool. If the muffins cool in the pan, the nut topping may stick to the pan and make it very difficult to remove them. If this happens, pop the muffins back into a 350°F oven for a minute to soften the molasses. These muffins are best eaten the day they're made. They can also be kept in an airtight container for up to 2 days.

Note: To encourage even baking and to allow each muffin enough room to have an individual dome top, fill alternate cups in a 24-cup tin, or use two 12-cup tins.

oat

Oat flour is the pale color of old pearls, and quite sweet. Like the oats the flour is ground from, it has a mild, milky taste that can blend into the background, neutral enough to complement a variety of ingredients. The Scots, who have long used oats as a staple grain, use it for oatmeal, cakes, and scones, where the grain pairs beautifully with fruit, cream, milk, and butter. Oats and oat flour partner particularly well with chocolate—as anyone who has ever stirred chocolate into oatmeal cookie dough will cheerfully attest.

Ground from groats (kernels), oat flour has a slight chewiness to it. What it doesn't have is gluten, so it needs to be mixed with other flours to avoid gumminess. Depending on the recipe, oat flour combines very well with all-purpose or whole-wheat flour, or a combination, as the wheat flours provide the necessary structure.

Oats have been a primary food grain for both humans and livestock for thousands of years. The grain has a thick, inedible outer husk that is first removed; the whole grains are then processed into groats, which are then steel-cut or steamed and rolled. This latter form is how we usually find oats, marketed as "old-fashioned rolled oats," or oatmeal. "Quick" oats are the same as old-fashioned, simply cut smaller and often rolled thinner for faster cooking. Rolled oats are usually steamed and rolled whole grains, although some products have had the bran removed before rolling—check the label on the package, or buy them from a whole-grain source if you have that option.

Since there are so many forms of oats on the market, try using more than one of them in a single recipe. Develop a cookie or a muffin with oat flour, then add rolled oats to the batter for the chewy bite they impart. Turn a handful of rolled oats into a streusel, then grind up more of them to give a chewy texture to a coffee cake or bread. Try toasting the oats first to give them a golden color and a pronounced nutty flavor—toast the oats plain or with a nub of butter.

If you can't find oat flour easily, try making your own. Just put rolled oats (make sure that they're whole-grain rolled oats and not instant) into a food processor or spice grinder and grind them until they're the grade you want. Depending on your equipment, you probably won't get a superfine flour, but it will work nonetheless.

Ginger Peach **Muffins**

Butter for the tins
2 tablespoons plus 1 teaspoon
grated fresh ginger

PEACH TOPPING:
1 large or 2 small peaches,
ripe but firm
1 tablespoon unsalted butter
1 tablespoon honey

DRY MIX:
1 cup oat flour
3/4 cup all-purpose flour
1/2 cup whole-wheat flour
1/4 cup sugar
1/4 cup dark brown sugar
1 teaspoon baking powder
1 teaspoon baking soda
3/4 teaspoon kosher salt

WET MIX:
3 ounces (3/4 stick) unsalted
butter, melted and cooled
slightly
3/4 cup whole milk
1/2 cup sour cream
1 egg
3 tablespoons finely chopped
crystallized ginger

Muffins are the cornerstone of everyday baking—at least in my kitchen—and they come together quickly, usually with just two bowls and a spatula. These muffins require a sauté pan too, but they're worth the extra washing up—they are among my favorites! Ripe peaches, cooked briefly in ginger syrup, are spooned over muffins made with soft, mellow oat flour and minced candied ginger. Be sure to use peaches that are slightly tart and not so ripe that they'll break apart in the sauté pan. And let them cool before eating the muffins, as oat flour is a bit moist when warm.

1. Place a rack in the middle of the oven and preheat to 350°F. Rub muffin tins with a 1/3-cup capacity with butter.
2. Grate the ginger into a large bowl. Some will be used for the topping and the rest for the batter.
3. For the topping, halve the peach, remove the pit, and slice the halves into slices about 1/4 inch thick. Add the butter, honey, and 1 teaspoon of the grated ginger to a medium-size skillet. Place the skillet over a medium flame to melt the mixture, stirring to combine. Cook until the syrup begins to bubble, about 2 minutes. Add the peaches, toss the pan to coat them with the syrup, and set aside.
4. Sift the dry ingredients into a large bowl, pouring back into the bowl any grain or other ingredients that may remain in the sifter. Add the wet ingredients to the bowl with the grated ginger and whisk until thoroughly combined. Using a spatula, mix the wet ingredients into the dry ingredients and gently combine.
5. Scoop the batter into 9 muffin cups, using a spoon or an ice cream scoop. The batter should be slightly mounded above the edge. Toss the pan of peaches to coat them with the pan juices. Lay one slice of peach over each of the muffins, tucking a second slice partway into the batter. Any extra peaches are delicious over yogurt or ice cream. Spoon the pan juices over the peaches.
6. Bake for 24 to 28 minutes, rotating the pans halfway through. The muffins are ready to come out when they smell nutty, their bottoms are golden in color (twist a muffin out of the pan to check), and the edges of the peaches are caramelized. Take the tins out of the oven, twist each muffin out, and place it on its side in the cup to cool. This ensures that the muffin stays crusty instead of getting soggy. These muffins are best eaten the same day they are made. They can also be kept in an airtight container for up to 2 days, or frozen and reheated.

Note: To encourage even baking and to allow each muffin enough room to have an individual dome top, fill alternate cups in a 24-cup tin, or use two 12-cup tins.

Oatmeal **Pancakes**

MAKES ABOUT 18

Butter for the pan

DRY MIX:
¾ cup oat flour
1 cup all-purpose flour
2 tablespoons sugar
2 teaspoons baking powder
¾ teaspoon kosher salt

WET MIX:
3 tablespoons unsalted
    butter, melted and cooled
    slightly
1¼ cups whole milk
1 cup cooked oatmeal (see
    Note below)
1 tablespoon unsulphured
    (not blackstrap) molasses
2 eggs

When I cook the things I make almost every day, like roasted vegetables or pots of oatmeal, I usually have a bit left over, or I make a bit extra on purpose. This foresight provides handy components for other dishes and saves time when making meals. A cup of cooked oatmeal adds moisture to breads and other baked goods. Stirred into this pancake batter, the oatmeal creates tenderness and a bit of chew. The molasses provides sweetness and enhances the creamy taste of the oats. These pancakes can be topped with your favorite syrup or jam, and they're fantastic with homemade Apple Butter (see page 198).

1. Sift the dry ingredients into a large bowl, pouring back into the bowl any bits of grain or other ingredients that may remain in the sifter. Whisk together the butter, milk, oatmeal, molasses, and eggs until thoroughly combined.
2. Using a spatula, gently fold the wet ingredients into the dry ingredients. For tender pancakes, it is important that you use a light hand while folding the batter with the spatula. The batter should be slightly thick, with a holey surface.
3. Although the batter is best if used immediately, it can sit for up to 1 hour on the counter or overnight in the refrigerator. When you return to the batter, it will be very thick and should be thinned, 1 tablespoon at a time, with milk—take great care to not overmix.
4. Heat a 10-inch cast-iron pan or griddle over medium heat until water sizzles when splashed onto the pan. Rub the pan generously with butter; this is the key to crisp, buttery edges, my favorite part of any pancake. Working quickly, dollop ¼-cup mounds of batter onto the pan, 2 or 3 at a time. Once bubbles have begun to form on the top side of the pancake, flip the pancake and cook until the bottom is dark golden-brown, about 5 minutes total. Wipe the pan with a cloth before griddling the next batch. Rub the pan with butter and continue with the rest of the batter. If the pan is too hot or not hot enough, adjust the flame accordingly to keep results consistent.
5. Serve the pancakes hot, straight from the skillet, spooning on a bit of apple butter or the topping of your choice.

Note: If you don't have any cooked oatmeal on hand, make a quick batch. In a small saucepan, bring 2 cups of water, 1 cup of whole rolled oats, and a pinch of salt to a boil. Simmer on low heat for about 5 minutes, then cool on the stove while you continue with this recipe. You'll have some extra oatmeal, which you can eat while you're cooking or save for another recipe.

Steel-Cut **Oatmeal**

SERVES 4

Steel-cut oats have an addictively chewy bite that puts them in a whole different category from standard rolled oats. During processing the oats are cut into small pieces rather than steamed and rolled flat. Their shape means they take longer to cook, but the flavor is absoutely worth the wait. Like rolled oats and many other grains, these oats are much more flavorful if you give them a quick toast in the pan before longer cooking. This brings out their natural sweet nuttiness and gives bite to the oats. Cream is an important ingredient in this dish—make it the best that you can find, preferably organic and definitely without any added thickeners. Add a spoonful of Pear Compote (see page 197) over the top.

1 tablespoon unsalted butter

1 cup steel-cut oats

1/4 teaspoon kosher salt

Organic cream, cold

1. Melt the butter in a 2-quart pot. Adjust the flame to medium and add the oats and salt. Stir the grains every minute or so for about 6 minutes. They need to be toasted about two shades darker than they are raw; keep a few raw grains on the counter next to you as a reference point. The oats are toasted when they reach a variety of colors from white to yellow to brown and your kitchen smells like popcorn.

2. Add 4 cups of water to the toasted oats and bring to a boil. Reduce the flame to low and simmer the grains, uncovered, for about 30 minutes, stirring the pot more frequently as the liquid thickens and the grains near the end of their cooking. The oatmeal should be tender, thick, and creamy.

3. Spoon the oatmeal evenly into 4 bowls and pour a desired amount of cold cream over each serving—I like a generous spoonful. If you made the pear compote, top each bowl with a quarter of the caramelized pears, about 4 slices each. Spoon any syrup remaining in the compote over the pears.

Granola **Bars**

2 ounces (¹/₂ stick) unsalted
   butter, plus extra to butter
   the pan and your hands

DRY MIX:

2 cups rolled oats
¹/₂ cup plus 1 tablespoon
   flaxseed meal
¹/₂ teaspoon cinnamon
¹/₂ cup raisins

SYRUP:

¹/₂ cup honey
¹/₄ cup dark brown sugar
1 tablespoon unsulphured
   (not blackstrap) molasses
1 teaspoon kosher salt

These bars, more cookie than health food, are loaded with oats and flaxseed meal. They'll satisfy a craving for an afternoon sweet or provide an energy boost while hiking or camping. Other rolled flakes like, rye, barley, or spelt can be substituted for the rolled oats, as can wheat germ or wheat bran for the flax seed meal. Toasting the oats in butter is crucial to the texture of the granola bars. This extra step results in a bar that is nutty and golden all the way through. I especially like the tartness that a mix of light and dark Flame raisins adds to the bars, but you can use whatever raisins you have on hand.

1. Preheat the oven to 325°F. Generously butter a 9-by-9-inch glass or metal baking dish.

2. Melt the butter in a heavy-bottomed pot that will hold 2 cups of oats with ample room for stirring. Adjust the flame to medium and stir the oats every minute or so for about 6 minutes. The oats need to be about two shades darker than they are raw; keep a few raw oats on the counter next to you as a reference point.

3. Pour the toasted oats into a large bowl. Wipe out the pot and set it aside to use again for the syrup. Add ¹/₂ cup of flaxseed meal and the cinnamon to the bowl.

4. Toss the raisins with the remaining tablespoon of flaxseed meal and chop finely. (Tossing the two together keeps the raisins from sticking to your knife.) Add them to the oat mixture.

5. To make the syrup, measure the honey, brown sugar, molasses, and salt into the reserved pot. Place it over a medium flame, stir to combine, and cook the syrup until evenly boiling, about 6 minutes. Resist the temptation to remove it early—boiling the syrup gives these granola bars real chew.

6. Pour the syrup over the oat mixture, making sure to use a spatula to scrape every last bit out. Then use the spatula to coat every flake with syrup. This means going over and over, tossing and scraping the oats together. Scrape the granola mixture into the prepared pan.

7. To form the bars, butter your hands and press the oats firmly and evenly into the pan.

8. Bake for 25 to 30 minutes, rotating the pan halfway through. The outer edge of the granola bars should be darker than the rest and the bars should have a beautiful sheen. Remove from the oven and let cool for 10 minutes. Cut the contents of the pan into quarters, for a total of 16 bars. Remove the bars from the pan and let cool before eating.

9. The granola bars can be eaten the day they're made, or kept in an airtight container for up to 3 days.

Oatmeal Sandwich Bread

Butter for the bowl and
   the pan

1 package active dry yeast

3 tablespoons unsulphured
   (not blackstrap) molasses

2$\frac{1}{2}$ cups whole-wheat flour

2 cups bread flour

1 cup rolled oats

2 ounces ($\frac{1}{2}$ stick) unsalted
   butter, melted and cooled
   slightly

1 tablespoon kosher salt

This is a moist, slightly sweet loaf, and it's fantastic for toast and sandwiches. The dough uses a method known as autolyse, in which all the ingredients except the salt are mixed together and then allowed to rest before kneading. This rest gives the flour time to absorb the water, yielding a wetter dough and a moister bread with a better, more irregular crumb. I make this dough in a mixer, as I find you don't need to use as much flour this way. If you prefer to make the bread by hand, knead the dough for about fifteen minutes, adding flour as needed.

1. Lightly butter a large bowl and a bread loaf pan about 9 by 5 by 3 inches. The dough can also be formed into a *boule* (round loaf) and baked on a baking sheet.

2. Add 2 cups of warm water, yeast, and molasses to the bowl of a standing mixer. Stir, allowing the yeast to bloom for about 5 minutes, until it begins to bubble. (If it doesn't, it may be inactive; throw it out and start over with a new package.)

3. To autolyse, measure the flours, oats, and butter into the bowl with the yeast mixture and stir together with a wooden spoon. Cover with a towel and let stand for 30 minutes.

4. Attach the bowl and the bread hook to the mixer, add the salt, and mix on medium speed for 6 minutes. The dough should slap around the sides without sticking to them. If the dough is sticking at any time during the mixing, add a tablespoon or two of bread flour until the dough comes away from the sides of the bowl. The dough should be soft and supple, slightly tacky, with a beautiful sheeting effect.

5. For the first rise, scrape the dough onto a lightly floured work surface and knead it a few times. Put the dough into the buttered bowl, cover with a towel, and leave it to rise for about 1 hour, or until it is doubled in size (see Sidebar).

6. To shape the dough, scrape the dough onto a lightly floured work surface. Press down on the dough, working it toward a square shape while depressing all of the bubbles. Fold the dough down from the top to the middle, then up from the bottom to the middle. Next bring the newly formed top and bottom edges together and pinch the seam in the middle, sealing the seam with your fingers. Pinch the sides together and roll the shaped dough back and forth, plumping it so that it's evenly formed and about the size of your loaf pan. Place the dough in the pan with the seam side down and press it gently into the corners of the pan.

7. For the second rise, cover the dough with a towel and let it rest in a warm place for

Proofing

A dough is proofed once it has fully risen. How can you tell if a dough is proofed? Gently push a floured finger into the dough. If it springs back, the dough needs to proof longer. If a dimple remains, move on to the next step.

about 1 hour, or until the dough rises to half again its size or puffs up barely or just over the edge of the pan. While the dough is rising, preheat the oven to 400°F.

8. When the dough has finished its final rise, sprinkle the top of the loaf with oats or bran, if desired.

9. Bake for about 40 minutes, rotating halfway through. The loaf is ready when the top crust is as dark as molasses and the bottom crust is dark brown. To see if the bread is ready, give the top of the loaf a thump to see if it sounds hollow. If the hollow sound isn't there and the bread isn't quite dark enough, bake for another 5 minutes. Remove the loaf from the pan and cool on a baking rack, preferably for a few hours, so that the crumb doesn't collapse when you cut into it and the flavor can develop.

Maple Oat **Waffles**

2 ounces (½ stick) butter,
   melted, for the waffle iron

DRY MIX:
½ cup oat bran
1 cup oat flour
2 cups all-purpose flour
1 tablespoon baking powder
1 teaspoon kosher salt

WET MIX:
2 cups cold whole milk
4 eggs, separated
½ cup maple syrup
2 teaspoons pure vanilla
   extract
1 tablespoon sugar

Oats and maple syrup are a natural breakfast combination. Here the syrup is stirred into the batter and used in place of sugar, and two grades of oats are used—bran and flour. The oat bran is soaked in warm milk to soften before being stirred into the batter. After the batter is stirred together, egg whites are whipped separately and then folded into the thick batter for loft and tenderness. One thing that's crucial to the success here, even more than in other waffle recipes: Butter the waffle iron generously, as a crisp crust really makes the difference in these waffles.

1. Turn the waffle iron to its highest setting. Even if you don't usually heat it this high, these waffles come out best when cooked at high heat.
2. Pour the oat bran into a small bowl. Bring 1 cup of the milk to just shy of a boil. Add the hot milk to the oat bran and stir, then set aside to soften while you gather the rest of the ingredients.
3. Sift the dry ingredients into a large bowl, pouring back into the bowl any bits of grain or other ingredients that may remain in the sifter.
4. Put the egg whites into the clean bowl of a standing mixer and the yolks into a medium bowl. Add the maple syrup and vanilla to the egg yolks and whisk until thoroughly combined.
5. Add the remaining 1 cup of milk to the oat bran—the cold milk will cool the lingering heat of the bran. Pour the oat mixture into the maple syrup mixture and stir to combine.
6. Using a spatula, add the wet ingredients to the dry ingredients and gently combine. The batter will still have fine

lumps throughout; resist the urge to mix them in.

7. To whip the egg whites, attach the mixing bowl and the whip to the mixer and turn the mixer to high speed. As the whites whip, they will become frothy and begin to increase in volume. Add 1 tablespoon sugar. Next they will turn thick but very soft. Continue whipping until they are fluffy and glossy and hold their peaks, like clouds or cotton candy, about 3 minutes total. If they are overwhipped, they'll crack and look mealy. If that happens, throw them out and start over.

8. Scrape half of the egg whites into the batter, stirring and folding gently so as not to deflate the air in the whites. Add the remaining half of the egg whites, and fold gently to combine. The egg whites should be entirely incorporated into the batter and the batter should be quite fluffy.

9. This light batter needs to be griddled on the waffle iron just as soon as you finish mixing it; it will deflate quickly if left to sit, chilled or otherwise.

10. Brush the waffle iron generously with butter. Using a ladle or measuring cup, scoop $1/2$ cup of batter onto the spaces of the iron. Promptly close, and listen for the iron to sigh as the batter begins to cook. The smell wafting from the iron starts out like a freshly kneaded loaf of bread, then becomes toasty. Remove the waffle when the indicator light shows that it is done, or when a quick peek shows that it has turned a dark golden-brown, 4 to 6 minutes. Remove the hot waffle with a fork, and repeat with the remaining batter.

11. These waffles are best eaten hot, right off the iron, with a thin slab of butter melting on top and maybe a bit of jam.

Seeded Granola

Butter for the baking sheets
or roasting pan

DRY MIX:

1 cup raw pumpkin seeds

4 cups whole rolled oats

1 cup raw sunflower seeds

1/2 cup wheat germ

1/4 cup flaxseeds

2 tablespoons brown sesame
seeds

1 tablespoon black sesame
seeds

1 tablespoon poppy seeds

1/2 teaspoon cayenne powder

SYRUP:

1/2 cup honey

1/2 cup dark brown sugar

3 ounces (3/4 stick) unsalted
butter

1 teaspoon kosher salt

After seeing an amber-colored brittle embedded with various seeds at Latin markets, I was inspired to create a granola that focused on seeds rather than nuts. In this recipe six kinds of seeds are blended with oats and a little wheat germ. A hint of cayenne gives the granola an addictive finish. Buying all the seeds in this recipe can get expensive, so feel free to adjust the recipe to fit your pantry.

1. Preheat the oven to 325°F. Spread the pumpkin seeds onto a baking sheet and bake until toasty and light golden-brown, about 18 minutes. (Remember that they will toast more in the oven when the granola bakes.) Butter two baking sheets or a large roasting pan.

2. Measure the dry ingredients, including the toasted pumpkin seeds, into a large bowl. Toss them all together with your hands.

3. To make the syrup, measure the honey, brown sugar, butter, and salt into a small heavy-bottomed saucepot. Place it over a medium flame, stir once, and cook until the syrup comes to an even boil, about 6 minutes. (This means that even the center of the syrup needs to be bubbling.) Resist the temptation to pull it off early—boiling the syrup gives the granola its crunchy, glazed crust.

4. As soon as the syrup has boiled, immediately pour it over the oat mixture, using a spatula to scrape every last bit out. Use the spatula to coat every flake with syrup. This means going over and over, tossing and scraping the oats together. Scrape the granola evenly over the prepared baking sheets or roasting pan, spreading it in a single, clumpy layer on each surface.

5. Bake for 10 minutes. Remove the sheets from the oven, close the oven door to retain the heat, and scrape the outer edges of the granola towards the center and the center out to the edges. Put the top sheet on the bottom rack and the bottom sheet on the top rack to ensure even baking, and repeat the baking and scraping a second and third time, for a total of 30 minutes. I prefer my granola on the darker end of the spectrum; if you don't, you might want to take the granola out after 5 to 6 minutes of the last bake.

6. Remove the sheets from the oven and allow the granola to cool thoroughly on the pans; this will allow small clumps to form. It will keep, stored in an airtight container, for at least 1 week.

Note: Baking granola is easiest in a pan with a rim, to contain the many loose ingredients. If your baking sheets have rims, use those; otherwise use a large roasting pan on the center rack of the oven. The granola needs a lot of surface area for even baking, so resist the temptation to bake all the granola on one baking sheet.

quinoa

Quinoa (pronounced KEEN-wa, from the Quechua kinwa) is a fascinating plant, a species of goosefoot indigenous to Peru and considered sacred by the Incas. Quinoa is capable of withstanding very high altitudes and of producing thousands of tiny edible seeds. Although you can find red quinoa, most is pale beige, and the flour ground from these seeds is light yellow. It has a flavor that can taste a bit like sesame or, when baked into a cookie, distinctly of peanut butter.

Baking with quinoa flour took some practice. Its flavor, earthier than that of many other whole-grain flours, can be a bit overwhelming at first. In fact, it first smelled like a bag of dirt to me and it took me a while to get used to it. Now it doesn't seem so strong—in fact, I find myself reaching for the quinoa flour for its distinctive taste.

Baking with quinoa flour can be a real pleasure. Paired with fruit and nuts, as in the Banana Walnut Cake in this chapter, the strawlike flavor of the quinoa isn't as pronounced. Hearty flavors like roasted beets are a fantastic match for quinoa, because the assertive qualities of both come together in the bowl, as in the recipe for Quinoa and Beet Pancakes.

The flavor of quinoa seeds is less pronounced than the flour, so instead of relying on them for flavor, I use them for the delightful pop that they add to a recipe. When cooking with quinoa seeds, it's important to note that the seeds need to be thoroughly rinsed before using to remove the saponin, a bitter protective coating. This is a simple process, except for the fact that the seeds are so small they'll drain through the holes of colanders, so use a fine-mesh sieve or place a few layers of cheesecloth in your colander when you do this.

Toasted first in a sauté pan (or not—this step is optional), then simmered for 15 minutes in boiling water, quinoa is a fantastic addition to salads, soups, or the Honeyed Quinoa Crêpes in this chapter, which combine cooked quinoa with a batter made from its flour.

When whole quinoa is cooked, the little tail of the germ spirals out of the seed, which is a visual indicator that the quinoa is done. As with other grains, be careful not to overcook. Because the seeds are so small and delicate, quinoa can go from nicely al dente to a panful of mush in just a few minutes. So watch for the spiraling germ and taste a few seeds to make sure they're still a bit chewy.

Quinoa **Porridge**

SPICED MILK:

1 cup heavy cream

1 cup whole milk

2 cinnamon sticks

1 teaspoon freshly grated
   nutmeg

1/2 teaspoon allspice

8 cardamom pods

2 teaspoons dark brown
   sugar

1/8 teaspoon kosher salt

QUINOA:

1 cup quinoa

1/3 cup currants

1/4 teaspoon kosher salt

FINISH:

Squash and Apple Compote
   (see page 195), optional

In the fall, when the mornings become overcast and foggy and the apples and squash are piling up at the farmers' market, I like to head to the kitchen to make this homey, rustic dish. A great source of breakfast protein, this porridge is satisfying alone, but it's even better with a spoonful of jam or compote.

1. To make the spiced milk, smash the cardamom pods with the back of a pan or the side of a knife. In a small saucepan, combine the cream, milk, spices, brown sugar, and salt. Bring the mixture to a boil, immediately turn the heat off, and leave the milk to steep, about 20 minutes.

2. Using a fine-mesh strainer or sieve, rinse the quinoa under cold water to remove any bitter residue. Place 2 cups of water, the quinoa, currants, and salt in a medium saucepan and bring to a boil. Reduce the flame to low and simmer, uncovered, until the quinoa is tender and tails spiral out of the grains, 12 to 15 minutes. Move the pan to a cooler spot on the stove and cover with a lid.

3. Strain the spiced milk into the quinoa without pressing the mixture in the strainer, so as to avoid any sediment passing through. Bring the porridge to a boil over a medium flame and simmer until the pudding has thickened slightly, about 4 minutes.

4. Divide the porridge evenly among 6 bowls and, if desired, top each bowlful with a large spoon of compote.

Honeyed Crêpes

MAKES 14

Unlike the other crêpes in this book, which are made with only whole-grain flours, here the quinoa flour is combined with an equal amount of all-purpose flour to temper the strong, earthy flavor. Cooked whole quinoa provides texture, even a little pop. (You'll have extra quinoa, which you can save for another use.) Drizzled with a mild honey or filled with Pear Compote (see page 197), these crêpes are great for breakfast or dessert.

Butter for the pan

QUINOA:
1 cup quinoa
Pinch of salt

BATTER:
$1/2$ cup quinoa flour
$1/2$ cup all-purpose flour
$1/2$ teaspoon kosher salt
$1^1/2$ cups whole milk
2 tablespoons unsalted butter, melted and cooled slightly
2 eggs

1. Bring 2 cups of water to a boil. Meanwhile, using a fine-mesh strainer or sieve, rinse the quinoa under cold water to remove any bitter residue. Add the quinoa and pinch of salt to the boiling water. Cover, reduce the flame to low, and cook until the quinoa is tender, 10 to 12 minutes, or until the grains are tender and tails are spiraling out of the grain. Cool and reserve.

2. In the order listed, measure the flours, salt, milk, butter, and eggs into a blender. Blend the batter until it is smooth and free of clumps, about 15 seconds. Leave the batter to stand at room temperature for about 1 hour.

3. After the crêpe batter has rested, stir in 1 cup cooled quinoa.

4. Heat an 8-inch cast-iron or nonstick pan over medium-high heat until a splash of water sizzles when it hits the pan. Rub the pan with butter. Hold the pan at an angle so that the handle is close to your body and tilted up, with the edge across from the handle tilted down toward the flame.

5. Using a 2-ounce ladle or $1/4$-cup measuring cup, scoop up some batter. Pour the batter just off-center in the pan and quickly swirl it around, aiming for one circular motion that creates a thin, even spread of batter in the pan. Do not add more batter to make up for empty space.

6. Cook the crêpe for about 1 minute, until the batter begins to bubble, leaving pinprick holes on the surface, and the edges begin to brown. Slide a metal spatula or spoon along the edge to loosen the crêpe, pinch the edge, and flip the crêpe over in one motion. Cook for 45 seconds longer, or until the crêpe is speckled brown and crisp around the edges. Remove to a plate, with the pretty side facing up.

7. The crêpes are best eaten straight from the pan after being folded in half and then in half again, making frilly-edged triangles. Serve with a drizzle of honey.

8. If the crêpes are made in advance, lay them individually on a baking sheet to toast in a 400°F oven for 5 or 6 minutes until they are warm, tender in the middle, and crisp on the edges. The crêpes can also be warmed individually in a pan. Crêpes can also be frozen, with parchment between each crêpe and wrapped tightly in plastic.

Quinoa and **Beet** Pancakes

Butter for the pan
3 medium-small red beets

DRY MIX:
1/2 cup quinoa flour
1/2 cup whole-wheat flour
1 cup all-purpose flour
3 tablespoons dark brown
   sugar
1 tablespoon baking powder
3/4 teaspoon kosher salt

WET MIX:
1 1/2 cups whole milk
1/3 cup plain yogurt
3 tablespoons unsalted
   butter, melted and cooled
   slightly
1 egg

These brilliantly pink breakfast pancakes were one of the first recipes I developed for the book. The beets are roasted until they caramelize to bring out their natural sweetness. Their earthy flavor pairs beautifully with the strawlike quality of quinoa flour. Making these pancakes is even easier if you plan ahead and roast beets for dinner, saving some leftovers for this recipe. If you want to serve these pancakes as a savory dish, serve them like blini, with smoked fish and sour cream, and cut the amount of brown sugar to 1 tablespoon.

1. Preheat the oven to 400°F. Place the beets in a glass or metal baking dish with about 1/2 cup water in the bottom. Cover with aluminum foil and roast until very tender, about 1 hour. Cool, peel, and purée the beets in a food processor or blender until smooth. You will need 1/2 cup of beet purée (any remaining purée can be frozen for another time).

2. Sift the dry ingredients into a large bowl, pouring back into the bowl any bits of grain or other ingredients that may remain in the sifter.

3. In a medium bowl, whisk together the milk, yogurt, melted butter, egg, and 1/2 cup of beet purée until smooth. Using a spatula, add the wet ingredients to the dry ingredients and gently combine. The batter should be the consistency of lightly whipped cream and crimson in color.

4. Although the batter is best if used immediately, it can sit for up to 1 hour on the counter or overnight in the refrigerator. When you return to the batter, it will be very thick and should be thinned, 1 tablespoon at a time, with milk—take great care not to overmix.

5. Heat a 10-inch cast-iron pan or griddle over medium heat until water sizzles when splashed onto the pan. Rub the pan generously with butter; this is the key to crisp, buttery edges, my favorite part of any pancake. Working quickly, dollop 1/4-cup mounds of batter onto the pan, 2 or 3 at a time. Once bubbles have begun to form on the top side of the pancake, flip it over and cook until the bottom is dark golden-brown, about 5 minutes total. Wipe the pan with a cloth before griddling the next batch. Rub the pan with butter and continue with the rest of the batter. If the pan is too hot or not hot enough, adjust the flame accordingly to keep results consistent.

6. Serve the pancakes hot, straight from the skillet, with a pitcher of warm maple syrup, encouraging your guests to pour as they please.

Quinoa **Cookies**

Butter for the baking sheets

DRY MIX:
2$\frac{1}{2}$ cups all-purpose flour
$\frac{1}{2}$ cup quinoa flour
2 teaspoons kosher salt
1$\frac{1}{2}$ teaspoons baking powder
1 teaspoon baking soda
2 teaspoons freshly grated
  nutmeg
1$\frac{1}{2}$ cups old-fashioned oats
1 cup quinoa flakes

WET MIX:
8 ounces (2 sticks) cold
  unsalted butter, cut into
  small pieces
1 cup dark brown sugar
1 cup sugar
2 tablespoons unsulphured
  (not blackstrap) molasses
2 eggs
2 teaspoons pure vanilla
  extract

FINISH:
$\frac{3}{4}$ cup quinoa flakes

This recipe began as a traditional oatmeal pecan cookie. Until one day, as I reached for the pecans in my cupboard, I noticed the jar of quinoa flakes—which I'd picked up out of curiosity at my local health-food store—sitting on the shelf. So I replaced some of the rolled oats in my cookie recipe with quinoa flakes and threw in a handful of quinoa flour to boost the flavor. The resulting accidental cookie recipe became one of my favorites. It tastes strikingly like a peanut butter cookie, but with a faint hint of sesame.

1. Place two racks in the upper and lower thirds of the oven and preheat to 350°F. Rub two baking sheets with butter.
2. Sift the dry ingredients into a large bowl, pouring back into the bowl any bits of grain or other ingredients that may remain in the sifter. Measure the oats and the quinoa flakes into a separate bowl.
3. Add the butter and sugars to the bowl of a standing mixer. Attach the paddle and mix on low speed until the butter and sugars are just blended, about 2 minutes. Use a spatula to scrape down the sides and the bottom of the bowl. Add the eggs, one at a time, mixing on high speed for 1 minute after each addition. Scrape down again. Mix in the molasses and vanilla. Add the flour mixture to the bowl and mix on low speed until the flour is barely combined, about 1 minute. Add the oats and 1 cup of quinoa flakes, again mixing on low speed and scraping down the sides and the bottom of the bowl (see Sidebar). This is a crumbly dough that will come together when the balls are formed.
4. For the finish, place the quinoa flakes into a shallow bowl. Scoop balls of dough about 3 tablespoons in size and roll them in the flakes. Place the cookies on the baking sheets, leaving about 3 inches between them.
5. Bake the cookies for 15 to 18 minutes, rotating halfway through. The cookies will be evenly golden brown. Transfer the cookies to a wire rack and let cool. These cookies are best eaten the day that they're made. They'll keep in an airtight container for up to 3 days.
6. If you aren't going to bake the batter all at once, shape the remaining dough into balls and coat them with the quinoa flakes— they'll adhere better and can be stored in the refrigerator for up to 1 week.

Cookie Dough

No matter how well you scrape down the sides of the bowl when making batter, there is often a small pocket of butter or unmixed ingredients at the very bottom. Rather than overmixing the dough, I stop the mixer, scrape the batter out onto a work surface, and use my hands to fully incorporate all the ingredients. A properly mixed dough ensures that your cookies bake uniformly.

Banana Walnut **Cake**

Ripe bananas can be cloying, but they're great for baking. In this recipe the fruit is paired with quinoa flour and walnuts to temper its sweetness. This is a homey cake, with a humble, old-fashioned quality that makes it a hit at school bake sales—or just around the kitchen, where I often find myself standing at the stove, slicing off wedges to have with a cup of tea.

1. Position a rack in the middle of the oven and preheat to 350°F. Rub a 9-inch round cake pan with butter.
2. Measure the walnuts onto a baking sheet and toast in the oven until light golden-brown and fragrant, about 15 minutes. Set aside to cool.
3. Sift the dry ingredients into a large bowl, pouring back into the bowl any bits of grain or other ingredients that may remain in the sifter, and set aside. Grind 1 cup of the toasted, cooled walnuts in a food processor, about 15 seconds. With a sharp knife, finely chop the remaining cup of walnuts and reserve. The chopped nuts will be added later as a topping.
4. Add the butter and sugars to the bowl of a standing mixer. Attach the bowl and the paddle and mix on medium-high speed until light and creamy, about 3 minutes. Using a spatula, scrape down the sides and the bottom of the bowl. Add the bananas and mix on medium speed for about 30 seconds, or until the bananas are broken down. Add the eggs, one at a time, and mix on medium speed, until thoroughly combined. Add the sour cream and vanilla and mix until combined. Again, scrape down the sides and the bottom of the bowl.
5. Add the ground walnuts and the dry ingredients to the mixing bowl and mix on low speed until just combined. Remove the bowl from the mixer, scrape down the sides, and stir the batter until uniformly combined.
6. Using a spatula, scrape the batter into the buttered pan and smooth the top. Sprinkle the chopped walnuts evenly over the top, out to the very edges.
7. Bake for 50 to 60 minutes, rotating the pan halfway through, until the cake is golden brown and springs back when lightly touched, or a skewer inserted in the center comes out clean. Allow the cake to cool in the pan. It should be eaten at room temperature. Wrapped tightly in plastic, the cake can be kept for up to 3 days.

Butter for the pan
2 cups walnut pieces

DRY MIX:
$1/2$ cup quinoa flour
1 cup all-purpose flour
1 tablespoon baking powder
1 teaspoon kosher salt

WET MIX:
4 ounces (1 stick) cold unsalted butter, cut into $1/2$-inch pieces
$1/2$ cup dark brown sugar
$1/2$ cup sugar
3 ripe bananas, about $1^1/4$ pounds
2 eggs
$1/3$ cup sour cream
1 teaspoon pure vanilla extract

rye

I have to admit that I put off baking with rye flour until I had worked my way through the other whole-grain flours. I had read that it was difficult to work with, and I associated it with pumpernickel bread—dark, dense, and slightly gummy. So when I started baking with whole-grain rye flour, I was surprised to discover how beautifully subtle it is, and how easy it is to sift into recipes.

One of the reasons rye is often misunderstood—people usually either love it or hate it—is that there are so many variables at play. Loaves of rye bread are often made with caraway seeds, which is great if you like their strong anise flavor, not so great if you don't. Pumpernickel bread can contain all kinds of ingredients other than rye, like molasses, coffee, or even cocoa. Then there's the flour itself, which comes in many forms: light, medium, dark, and pumpernickel.

Whole-grain rye flour is actually quite mild and slightly milky, with a trace of maltiness and even caramel in the background. Without the caraway and other ingredients often found in commercial rye breads, there isn't any of the sour taste that people sometimes associate with rye. Actually, the flour is rather sweet.

That said, rye works best when combined with other flours, ideally all-purpose flour, as rye has less gluten and absorbs more water than wheat—hence its tendency to create breads that are dense and gummy if used in too great a quantity. I found that I most frequently used a one-to-one ratio of all-purpose and rye flours. In recipes where I wanted even more loft, as for a yeasted pretzel or a laminated Danish, I increased the ratio to two parts all-purpose to one part rye.

For the recipes in this book, I used dark rye flour that was milled from the entire grain. If you can't find whole-grain rye flour, your best bet is to use a dark rye flour, even if it's had part of the bran or germ removed, as it will have the best flavor.

Gentle and malty, rye flour pairs well with rich, sweet flavors like maple, dried cherries, dates, and ripe summer stone fruits—it's particularly good with apricots. It also provides the central flavor and the slightly chewy texture to a basic pretzel recipe.

To my surprise, rye flour provided the missing link in those recipes I couldn't quite figure out, like a tender yeasted sweet dough, a flaky pie crust, and muffin batters. It turned out to be the flour with the greatest range, and it went from being something I misunderstood to a staple in my pantry.

Cherry Hazelnut **Muesli**

1 cup whole raw hazelnuts,
skins on

1 teaspoon olive oil

1/2 teaspoon kosher salt

2 cups rye flakes

1/4 cup plus 1 tablespoon
wheat bran

1/2 cup quinoa flakes

Generous 1/3 cup dried
cherries

Generous 1/3 cup dried
cranberries

Muesli is a hearty Swiss breakfast cereal made of oats, nuts, and dried fruits. Like granola, it can include a wide variety of ingredients. Instead of cherries and hazelnuts, use any combination of nuts and dried fruits, or add different spices or grains to the mix. Make a batch of muesli and keep it in a jar on the counter. In the morning, pour organic whole milk into a bowl with the muesli and top with loads of fresh seasonal fruit and a sprinkle of salt (yes, salt—it brings out the flavors). Stir a spoonful of honey in, too.

1. Place the oven racks at the upper and lower thirds of the oven and preheat to 350°F. Toss the hazelnuts together with the oil and salt and spread them on a baking sheet. Toast for 16 to 18 minutes, stirring the nuts halfway through. The nuts should be fragrant and dark brown, but not burnt. Leave the skins from the nuts on for a rustic touch in both appearance and taste.

2. While the nuts are toasting, spread the rye flakes in a single layer on another baking sheet. Toast the rye flakes in the same oven simultaneously for 10 minutes, until golden and crunchy. Remove from the oven and let cool.

3. Once the nuts have cooled, roughly chop them, leaving a few whole. Add them to a large bowl along with the rye flakes, 1/4 cup wheat bran, and quinoa flakes.

4. Mix the cherries and cranberries with the remaining wheat germ, to prevent sticking. Chop them into halves or thirds, leaving some whole. Add them to the bowl and toss together with your hands.

5. The muesli can be eaten immediately, or you can wait until it's cooled completely and store it in an airtight container. It will keep for at least 2 weeks.

Zucchini **Bread**

Butter for the pan

2 tablespoons basil, about 12
   medium leaves
1 tablespoon mint, about 8
   medium leaves

WET MIX:
4 ounces (1 stick) unsalted
   butter
1/2 pound zucchini (about
   2 medium)
1/2 cup plain yogurt
2 eggs

DRY MIX:
1 cup rye flour
1 cup all-purpose flour
1/4 cup wheat germ
1/2 cup sugar
1 1/2 teaspoons baking
   powder
1/2 teaspoon baking soda
1/2 teaspoon kosher salt

Rye flour is a lot subtler than you might think, and its malt flavor pairs well with fresh herbs, in this case basil and mint. Grated zucchini is stirred into the batter for moisture and substance, as well as color. This bread was inspired by the sometimes overwhelming amount of zucchini in my garden. At the height of zucchini season, when it gets difficult to imagine what *else* to do with the stuff, try mixing up some of this bread. I especially like a slice with a nub of melted butter and a pot of mint tea.

1. Position a rack in the middle of the oven and preheat to 350°F. Lightly butter a standard bread loaf pan.
2. Pick the basil and mint leaves from their stems, roughly chop the leaves, and reserve. Melt the butter. Add the herbs to the butter to infuse their flavor while the other ingredients are being prepared.
3. Slice the ends off the zucchini. Grate the whole zucchini on the largest holes of a box grater into a large mixing bowl. Add the yogurt and eggs to the bowl and whisk thoroughly.
4. Sift the dry ingredients into another large mixing bowl, pouring back any bits of grain or other ingredients that may remain in the sifter. Scrape the butter with herbs into the zucchini mixture and stir together. Pour the zucchini mixture into the dry ingredients, gently folding until just combined. Scrape the batter into the prepared pan and smooth the top.
5. Bake for 60 to 70 minutes, rotating the pan halfway through. The cake should be dark golden-brown and spring back when lightly touched; a skewer inserted into the center should come out clean. Remove the cake from the oven and cool in the pan for 10 minutes. Then, invert the cake out of the pan and cool on a baking rack. The cake should be eaten at room temperature.
6. Wrapped tightly in plastic, it can be kept up to 3 days, even getting better the next day after the flavors have some time to meld together.

Rustic Rye **Dough**

This is the dough I use when I make free-form tarts, sometimes called "galettes." When I was at Campanile we called them "rustics"—hence the recipe's name. They're my favorite kind to make because you only need your hands to shape them, and the less contrived they come out, the better. The sweet, milky flavor of the rye flour pairs beautifully with fruit, as in Apricot Boysenberry Tarts (see page 152). The method for making this dough is similar to that for a rough puff pastry, a method I learned while working with Sherry Yard at Spago. It calls for letting a rough dough, made from chunks of butter and moist clumps of flour, rest in the refrigerator to give the gluten time to relax and the flour time to absorb the water. After an hour, the dough is rolled and folded a few times to create long "laminated" layers of butter throughout the dough, which give it its flakiness.

$3/4$ cup ice water

DRY MIX:

1 cup rye flour
1 cup all-purpose flour
1 tablespoon sugar
1 teaspoon kosher salt

WET MIX:

6 ounces ($1^1/_2$ sticks) cold
    unsalted butter
1 teaspoon apple cider
    vinegar

1. Sift the dry ingredients into a large bowl, adding back any bits of grain or other ingredients that may remain in the sifter. Cut the butter into $1/2$-inch pieces and add them to the dry mixture.

2. Rub the butter between your fingers, breaking it into smaller bits. Continue rubbing until the butter is in sizes ranging from peas to hazelnuts. The more quickly you do this, the more the butter will stay solid, which is important for the success of the recipe.

3. Add the vinegar and 8 tablespoons of ice water to the flour mixture. Working from the outer edge of the flour, mix the ingredients with your hands just to moisten the flour. The dough needs to come together as mostly one lump, with a few shaggy pieces. Squeeze the dough together to see if a ball forms. If it is too dry to come together, add additional ice water 1 tablespoon at a time.

4. Pile the dough onto a sheet of plastic wrap, sprinkle a few drops of water over the top, wrap tightly, and chill for a minimum of 1 hour or overnight.

5. Unwrap the dough onto a floured surface. Pat the dough into a square, then use a rolling pin to roll it into a rectangle about $8^1/_2$ by 11 inches. The dough will be crumbly and rough around the edges, but don't add more flour or water, as it will come together during the rolling.

6. For the first turn, fold the dough into thirds like a letter. The seam should be on the left side. Turn the dough so that the seam is at the top and parallel to your body.

7. For the second turn, again roll the dough into an $8^1/_2$-by-11-inch rectangle and repeat the previous step.

8. For the third turn, repeat the previous step, then wrap the dough in plastic and chill for 1 hour or up to 3 days before using.

Apricot Boysenberry Tarts

Parchment for the
baking sheets

1 recipe Rustic Rye Dough
(see page 149)
1¼ cups Apricot Jam
(see page 188)
2 pounds ripe apricots
2 to 4 tablespoons sugar,
depending on the
sweetness of the fruit
1½ cups boysenberries

FINISH:

1 egg
¼ cup sugar
½ teaspoon cinnamon

During that brief moment at the farmers' market when apricots and boysenberries overlap, you'll find me in the kitchen making these rustic tarts. Both fruits are slathered in homemade jam, tucked into rye dough, and baked until dark and crusty. Freeze the tart before baking so that it keeps its shape—and while you're at it, freeze some extra tarts for later.

1. Cut the apricots in half and discard the pits. Put the apricots into a large bowl. Add the sugar and stir to coat. Pour ½ cup of apricot jam over the top and stir again. The apricots should be lightly coated, with just a dab of jam sticking to the center of each.

2. In a separate bowl, gently stir ¼ cup of jam with the boysenberries, being mindful to keep the berries whole.

3. To shape the dough, divide it in half. Keep one half chilled while the other is being shaped. Flour the work surface and roll the dough into a rough circle about 15 inches in diameter. Transfer the circle of dough to a baking sheet lined with parchment.

4. To form the tart, smear ¼ cup of jam at the bottom of the tart. Pile half of the apricots and half of the boysenberries into the center of the dough, tucking the boysenberries into the nooks and crannies of the apricots. Fold an edge of the dough toward the center to cover the fruit; about 3 inches of crust should be showing. Continue folding the edge of the dough toward the filling and over, to create folds. Each one will look different, and that is just how it should be.

5. Once the tart is formed, it should be about 9 inches in diameter. Using the same procedure, shape the second tart on a separate parchment-lined baking sheet, smearing the crust with the remaining ¼ cup jam. Freeze both tarts for a minimum of 1 hour.

6. While the tarts are freezing, preheat the oven to 350°F.

7. Stir the sugar and cinnamon together. Whisk the egg into an egg wash (see Sidebar, page 105). Take the baking sheets out of the freezer. Brush the edges of the dough with the egg wash, and sprinkle half of the cinnamon sugar evenly over each of the tarts, on both the crust and the fruit. Don't skimp, it creates a great crust.

8. Bake for 60 to 70 minutes, rotating the pans halfway through. The tarts are ready when the crusts are dark golden-brown and blistering, the jam is bubbling, and perhaps some juice has run from the tart and caramelized on the parchment paper.

9. Serve the tarts warm from the oven or later that same day. The unbaked tarts will keep, well wrapped and frozen, for up to 1 month.

Soft Rye **Pretzels**

These pretzels are soft, chewy, and flavorful, with a slight sourness that comes from boiling the pretzels in a baking soda bath. The baking soda also gives the pretzels their traditional dark mahogany color. Be sure to boil only a few pretzels at a time and to use the bath for only a single batch of the recipe—otherwise the baking soda water reduces too far and leaves a metallic bite to the dough. A simple dusting of sea salt, especially flaky Maldon salt, is the best finish to these. Serve a basket of the pretzels with a pot of whole-grain mustard.

1. Measure the yeast into a large bowl. Heat 1½ cups of water in a small saucepan over low heat to a temperature that is warm to the touch, about 100°F, and pour it over the yeast. Add the honey and stir to combine. Add the flours and salt and stir again.

2. Dump the sticky dough onto a floured surface and knead. Add up to ½ cup all-purpose flour, as needed, until the dough is tacky but not sticky. Knead for about 12 minutes, or until the dough is soft and supple.

3. Lightly brush a large bowl with melted butter. Using a dough scraper, scrape the dough into the bowl, cover with plastic wrap or a towel, and let rise for about 1½ hours, or until doubled in size (see Sidebar, page 130).

4. While the dough is rising, place two racks at the top and bottom thirds of the oven and preheat to 450°F. Brush two baking sheets generously with butter.

5. Once the dough has doubled, gently pour it from the bowl onto a lightly floured surface. Cut the dough into 12 pieces. Take each piece of dough and roll it into a snake about 17 inches long, with thinly tapered ends. Don't flour your surface as you roll; the slight stickiness enables you to roll the dough out evenly and quickly. Form the dough into a pretzel shape by folding one-third of the left side over the center of the snake, and then one-third of the right side over the left. Place the shaped pretzels onto the prepared baking sheets. Let the pretzels proof (rise) for 15 to 20 minutes.

6. Meanwhile, for the bath, fill a large pot with 10 cups of water and bring it to a boil. Once the pretzels are proofed and the water is boiling, add the baking soda to the water.

7. To poach the pretzels, lift 2 or 3 pretzels, depending on the surface area of your pot, into the bath. Boil each side for 30 seconds, use a strainer to remove the pretzels, pat any excess water with a towel, and transfer them back onto the buttered baking sheets. Boil the remaining pretzels. Sprinkle liberally with salt.

8. Bake for 15 to 18 minutes, rotating the sheets halfway through. The pretzels should be dark mahogany in color. Transfer them to a rack to cool. These pretzels are best eaten the day they're made, ideally within the hour.

2 tablespoons unsalted
   butter, melted, for the
   bowl and the baking sheets

DOUGH:
1 package active dry yeast
1 tablespoon honey
1 cup rye flour
2½ cups all-purpose flour
1 tablespoon kosher salt

BATH:
½ cup baking soda

FINISH:
Coarse sea salt, such as
   Maldon

Crumble Bars

Butter for the pan

SHORTBREAD CRUST:
1/2 cup rye flour
1 cup all-purpose flour
1/3 cup dark brown sugar
1/2 teaspoon kosher salt
4 ounces (1 stick) unsalted
     butter, melted and cooled
1 teaspoon pure vanilla
     extract

CRUMBLE TOPPING:
1 cup whole rolled oats
3 tablespoons dark brown
     sugar
1/4 cup plus 2 tablespoons rye
     flour
1/4 cup all-purpose flour
3 tablespoons sugar
1 teaspoon kosher salt
3 ounces unsalted butter,
     melted and cooled

1 1/2 cups jam, fruit butter, or
     compote

This recipe may look long and involved, as it has three separate components. However, each one by itself is quite simple, and the components can all be made in advance and kept in the refrigerator or freezer until you're ready to bake the bars. In the summer, I love these bars slathered with Strawberry Jam (see page 190) and in the winter with Apple Butter (see page 198). If you don't have the time or ingredients to make those, open up a jar of some other homemade or purchased jam or compote. Rye flour, with its mild, sweet flavor, makes this recipe quite versatile, and it adapts easily to whatever fruit spread you have on hand.

1. Position a rack in the middle of the oven and preheat to 275°F. Rub a 9-inch springform pan with butter.

2. To make the shortbread crust, sift the flours, sugar, and salt into a large bowl, pouring back into the bowl any bits of grain or other ingredients that may remain in the sifter. Add the melted butter and vanilla and stir until thoroughly combined. Using your hands, press the dough evenly into the bottom of the buttered pan. Put the pan in the freezer for 30 minutes while you make the crumble topping.

3. Add all of the crumble ingredients except the melted butter to the bowl of a food processor and process until the oats are partially ground, about 5 seconds. Pour the mixture into a bowl. Add the melted butter and stir with your hands, squeezing the dough as you mix to create small crumbly bits. Set aside.

4. Bake the frozen shortbread until golden brown and firm when touched, 50 to 55 minutes. Remove the shortbread from the oven and increase the temperature to 350°F.

5. To assemble the crumble bars, spread 1 1/2 cups jam, fruit butter, or compote over the shortbread crust and top with the crumble, evenly sprinkling it over the surface and squeezing bits of it together to create irregular crumbles. Bake the bars for 50-55 minutes, until golden brown, rotating the pan halfway for even baking.

6. When the pan is cool enough to handle but still warm, run a sharp knife around the edge of the crumble bars to loosen any fruit that may have stuck to the pan while baking and remove the ring. Keep the crumble bars in the pan until they are completely cool, then cut them into wedges. These bars are best eaten the day that they're made. They'll keep in an airtight container for up to 2 days.

Banana Cereal **Muffins**

I cook a batch of oatmeal for my daughters almost every morning, but sometimes I vary the routine (slightly) by cooking multigrain cereal instead. These aren't rolled grains, but a variety of cracked grains. When I do this, I save back half a cup of the cooked cereal to make these muffins later in the week. Another option is to make a batch of cereal and freeze half-cup portions. Use the ripest, most freckled bananas you have, as that will give the most intense flavor to the muffins, as well as a moister crumb.

Butter for the tins

$1/2$ cup cracked-multigrain hot cereal, such as Bob's Red Mill

Pinch of salt

DRY MIX:

1 cup rye flour

1 cup all-purpose flour

$1^1/2$ teaspoons baking powder

$1/2$ teaspoon baking soda

1 teaspoon kosher salt

1 teaspoon cinnamon

WET MIX:

3 ounces ($3/4$ stick) cold unsalted butter

$1/4$ cup dark brown sugar

3 ripe bananas, about $1^1/4$ pounds

2 tablespoons unsulphured (not blackstrap) molasses

1 egg

1. Bring $1^1/2$ cups of water to a boil. Add the grains and salt and whisk to prevent any clumping. Reduce the flame to low and cook, uncovered, stirring occasionally, until the cereal is tender, 17 to 20 minutes. Cool and set aside $1/2$ cup of the cereal, saving the rest for another use.

2. Preheat the oven to 350°F. Rub muffin tins with a $1/3$-cup capacity with butter.

3. Sift the dry ingredients into a large bowl, pouring back into the bowl any bits of grain or any other ingredients that may remain in the sifter.

4. Add the butter and brown sugar to the bowl of a standing mixer. Attach the paddle and mix on high speed until the butter and sugars are light and creamy, about 2 minutes. Using a spatula, scrape down the sides and the bottom of the bowl. Add the bananas, molasses, egg, and the $1/2$ cup cooled cereal and mix on medium speed until thoroughly combined, about 1 minute.

5. Scrape down the sides and the bottom of the bowl. Add the dry ingredients and mix on low speed, blending until just combined.

6. Scoop the batter into 8 muffin cups, using a spoon or an ice cream scoop. The batter should be mounded above the edges of the cups.

7. Bake for 35 to 40 minutes, rotating the pans halfway through. The muffins are ready to come out when their bottoms are dark golden in color (twist a muffin out of the pan to check). Remove the tins from the oven, twist each muffin out, and place it on its side in the cup to cool. This ensures that the muffin stays crusty instead of getting soggy. These muffins are best eaten warm from the oven or later that same day. They can also be kept in an airtight container for up to 2 days, or frozen and reheated.

Note: To encourage even baking and to allow each muffin enough room to have an individual dome top, fill alternate cups in a 24-cup tin, or use two 12-cup tins.

Maple **Danish**

Butter for the baking sheets

DRY MIX:

1 cup rye flour

2 cups all-purpose flour

$1/4$ cup sugar

$1^1/2$ teaspoons kosher salt

6 ounces ($1^1/2$ sticks)
   unsalted butter, frozen

WET MIX:

1 package plus 1 teaspoon
   active dry yeast

$3/4$ cup whole milk, warmed
   to about 100°F

1 egg

FILLING:

3 tablespoons unsalted
   butter, softened to room
   temperature

$1/4$ cup maple sugar

2 tablespoons dark brown
   sugar

This recipe is all about technique. This doesn't mean that it is particularly difficult, merely that it has specific directions you'll want to follow closely. As in many pastry recipes, the condition and treatment of the butter is crucial. Here the butter is frozen before being grated, as it keeps the shreds of butter separate and prevents them from melting into the flour before the dough is baked. (Don't try this recipe on a very hot day.) When you stir the yeast mixture into the flour, be careful to do it briefly, barely combining the ingredients. When you master these techniques, the Danish will come out wonderfully flaky.

1. Sift the dry ingredients into a large bowl, pouring back into the bowl any bits of grain or other ingredients that may remain in the sifter. Using the large holes on a box grater, quickly grate the frozen butter into the dry mixture—this will ensure that the butter stays cold. With your hands, very briefly stir the strands of butter into the mix and then chill while you continue with the recipe.

2. Measure the yeast and warm milk into a small bowl. Stir and allow the yeast to bloom for about 5 minutes, or until the yeast begins to bubble. (If it doesn't, it may be inactive; throw it out and start over with a new package.) Add the egg and whisk thoroughly. Scrape the yeast mixture into the refrigerated dry mixture and stir to moisten the flour. There will still be some drier bits of dough; that's fine. Cover the dough with plastic wrap and chill overnight.

3. The next day, take the dough out of the refrigerator and scrape it onto a well-floured surface. It will be quite rough,

but don't worry; it will come together as you work with it.

4. Flour the top of the dough and use your hands to shape the dough into a rough square, pressing the loose bits together as you go. Using a rolling pin, roll the dough into a rectangle about 9 inches by 15 inches, keeping the longer side parallel to your body.

5. For the first turn, fold the rectangle of dough into thirds like a letter. Then turn the dough to the right once, so that the long edge of the dough is parallel to your body and the seam is at the top. As the dough is still quite rough, a metal bench scraper will help you lift the dough to make these folds.

6. Flour the surface and the dough and repeat the step above two more times, for a total of three turns. As you do the turns, the dough will become more cohesive and streaks of butter will begin to show throughout. The dough will also soften as the butter begins to warm and the yeast begins to react.

7. To shape the dough, cut it in half with a knife or a bench scraper. Roll each piece of dough into a 12-by-8-inch rectangle, keeping the shorter side parallel to your body. Rub the softened butter over the rectangles, dividing it equally between the two. Sprinkle the sugars evenly over the butter.

8. Roll up the dough, one rectangle at a time, starting at the shorter edge closer to you and keeping a tight spiral as you roll. Slice each log into 6 even slices and lay them on 2 buttered baking sheets, spiral side up, 6 to a sheet.

9. To proof, cover each baking sheet with a towel or plastic wrap and allow to rest in a warm area for 2 hours. While the dough is proofing, preheat the oven to 425°F. After 2 hours, the spirals will be slightly swollen but will not have doubled in size.

10. Bake for 15 to 18 minutes, rotating the sheets halfway through. The pastries are ready to come out of the oven when the sugars are caramelized and the tops of the Danish are golden-brown. These pastries are best eaten the day they're made, ideally within the hour.

spelt

Spelt is a grain with footprints in the Stone Age and fingerprints in the Old Testament, where it survived the plagues of Exodus for the simple reason that its season was later than that of flax and barley.

Ground to flour, it looks and acts like a milder version of the wheat flour to which it's closely related. Spelt has a slightly tart aroma but no trace of the bitterness that can come with many whole-wheat flours. It's also distinctly sweet.

The origins of spelt date to the Neolithic or Stone Age (circa 6000 B.C.E.), when wild or cultivated emmer mixed with indigenous wild grasses in the fertile area that is modern-day Iran. A variety that was the result of this cross-breeding, spelt, was then cultivated and distributed throughout Europe and Asia. It was a popular grain, hardy and nutritious, though with a tough outer husk that made it difficult to thresh. This tough husk eventually caused farmers to replace spelt with other grains that could be more easily—and less expensively—processed. Ironically, it's this covering that now makes spelt attractive to organic farmers, who appreciate the grain's resistance to disease and infestation.

Baking with spelt is extremely easy and satisfying, as it can be substituted directly for whole-wheat or all-purpose flour in most recipes. The sweetness of the flour complements additional flavors instead of overpowering them as some more assertive flours can do.

Spelt flour is quite water-soluble, which means that doughs and batters made with it will often absorb more liquid than with other flours. Therefore, when substituting spelt for other wheat flours in recipes, you may need to increase the amount of liquid that the recipe calls for.

Baked goods made with spelt have a soft and tender crumb, but with enough structure to hold up to additional ingredients, such as the generous amount of shredded carrots in the Carrot Muffins. The carrots also provide the additional moisture needed when baking with spelt flour.

If you were going to pick one whole-grain flour to start baking with, spelt flour, with its mild, sweet nature, would be the one.

Currant **Scones**

Butter for the baking sheets

DRY MIX:
1¼ cups spelt flour
1 cup all-purpose flour
2 tablespoons sugar
1 tablespoon baking powder
½ teaspoon kosher salt

WET MIX:
2 ounces (½ stick) cold
    unsalted butter, cut into
    ½-inch pieces
½ cup currants
1½ cups heavy cream

When I was a student, for a time, in Cambridge, England, I ate a currant scone every day of the semester. They were rough-dropped mounds, with crisp edges and studded with currants. When trying to recreate these scones in my kitchen, I reached for spelt flour. Its underlying hint of ripe fruit complements the sweetness of the currants. If you want more dried fruit, sprinkle a larger handful into the batter.

1. Position a rack in the middle of the oven and preheat to 400°F. Rub two baking sheets with butter. Sift the dry ingredients into a large bowl, pouring back into the bowl any grains or other ingredients that may remain in the sifter.
2. Add the butter to the dry ingredients. With your hands, work the butter, pinching it until the mixture resembles fine cornmeal. Add the currants and stir to combine. Pour the cream into the bowl and stir the ingredients just until the flour is moistened throughout.
3. Separate the dough into 9 mounds on the baking sheets, leaving about 4 inches between the mounds. Use your hands to break up any large heaps of dough and to tuck in the crumbs.
4. Bake for 18 to 20 minutes, rotating the pans halfway through. You'll know these scones are done when the tops and bottoms turn golden brown. The scones are best eaten warm from the oven or later that same day.

Spelt Pie **Dough**

There are three basic schools of thought about what makes flaky pie dough: butter, shortening, or both. For classic pie dough, I'm in the last camp. Technique also determines how flaky your crust will be. Here I use a method known as *fraisage*, in which you smear pea-size pieces of fat into the flour to create alternating layers of dough and fat. During baking, the fat melts, creating steam that lifts up the layers of dough, creating a very tender pastry—it's a simple step that creates an incredible crust. This dough is made with a combination of all-purpose and spelt flour, which adds creamy color and a mild, nutty flavor. It also provides a bit more texture, which can come in handy when you use this dough for jammy tarts or savory pies.

DRY MIX:

$1^{1}/_{3}$ cups spelt flour

$1^{1}/_{3}$ cups all-purpose flour

1 tablespoon sugar

1 teaspoon kosher salt

WET MIX:

4 ounces (1 stick) cold
unsalted butter

$^{1}/_{4}$ cup vegetable shortening
(such as Crisco)

$^{1}/_{2}$ cup ice water, as needed

1. Sift the dry ingredients into a large bowl, pouring back any grains or other ingredients that may remain in the sifter. Cut the butter into hazelnut-size pieces and add the butter and the shortening to the dry ingredients.

2. Rub the butter and shortening between your fingers, breaking them into smaller pieces until they are the size of peas. The more quickly you do this, the more the butter and shortening will stay solid, which is important for the success of the recipe.

3. Add $^{1}/_{4}$ cup of ice water to the flour-and-butter mixture and, working from the outer edge of the flour, mix the ingredients with your hands just to moisten the flour. The dough needs to come together as mostly one lump, with a few shaggy pieces. Squeeze a handful of dough to see if it is moist enough. If the dough is too dry to come together, add ice water 1 tablespoon at a time.

4. For the *fraisage*, dust a work surface with flour. Use a pastry scraper or a spatula to transfer the dough onto the work surface. Take a pinch of dough about 2 tablespoons in size, set it on the counter, and push the heel of your hand down toward the counter and away from you. You want to smear the dough, flattening and elongating the butter—this is what gives the baked crust a tender and very flaky crumb.

5. Repeat with the remaining dough, then separate the dough into 2 equal pieces. Wrap each piece in plastic and chill for a minimum of 1 hour or up to 3 days.

Summer Peach **Pie**

1 batch of Spelt Pie Dough
(see page 163), divided into
2 halves

4 pounds ripe peaches, about
12 large peaches

1/3 cup sugar

1 tablespoon cornstarch

1 tablespoon unsalted butter

FINISH:

1 egg for an egg wash

2 tablespoons sugar

1/2 teaspoon cinnamon

Peaches for pie should be just as ripe and flavorful as any peach you would eat out of hand. For the best pie, buy your peaches in season. Peaches are ripe when they smell fragrant, almost floral, and yield slightly to a gentle press of your thumb. For the pie, they are blanched, like tomatoes, to remove their skins. It's a quick step and one that's well worth the effort, as the skins slip off easily and you won't waste any of the fruit. Nectarines can be used in place of peaches and they don't need to be peeled.

1. To blanch the peaches, fill a large pot two-thirds full with water and bring to a boil. Meanwhile, slice an X into the bottom of each peach. When the water is at a rapid boil, lower 3 or 4 peaches into it. Count to 15, pull the peaches from the water with a slotted spoon or a strainer. Tap the bottoms on a towel to absorb excess water, and place the peaches in a large bowl. Blanch the remaining peaches, letting the water return to a boil each time.

2. Peel the peaches, cut them from their pits and slice them into 1-inch wedges. Put the wedges into a bowl, sprinkle them with sugar, and macerate for 30 minutes.

3. Strain the juice and measure out 1/3 cup. Whisk the cornstarch into the juice until smooth, and pour over the peaches.

4. Take one half of the dough from the refrigerator, and flatten into a disk.

5. Flour the work surface and, with a rolling pin, roll the dough into a circle roughly 14 inches in diameter. If the dough sticks, slide a pastry scraper under the dough and dust the surface with flour.

6. Fold the dough in half and then half again, to form a wedge. Transfer it to a 2-inch-deep pie dish and unfold. Press the dough into the dish, leaving some slack to allow for shrinkage during baking. Spoon the peaches into the dish, mounding them up in the center.

7. Remove the second disk of dough from the refrigerator and roll it out the same way, this time into a slightly smaller circle, about 12 inches in diameter. Fold this disk into a wedge, place it over the top of the pie, and carefully unfold it, pressing the dough onto the fruit with your hands. Trim the edges of the dough if necessary; then with your fingers, pinch the edges to seal them together, crimping or shaping the crust as you like. Freeze the pie for 45 minutes.

8. While the pie is freezing, preheat the oven to 375°F. Whisk the egg into an egg wash (see Sidebar, page 105), and in a separate small bowl stir the sugar and cinnamon together. After 45 minutes, take the pie out of the freezer, brush it with the egg wash, and sprinkle the top with the cinnamon sugar. Cut slits around the center of the top crust.

9. Bake for about 1 hour, placing a piece of foil over the top crust at the very end of baking if the crust is getting too brown. The pie is done when it's browned and the peach juice is bubbling out from the edges. Cool the pie slightly on the stovetop and eat it warm from the oven or later that same day. Wrapped tightly in plastic, the pie will keep for 2 days.

Carrot Muffins

Scented with allspice and laced with shreds of carrot, these muffins strike a balance between sweetness and spice. The streusel topping adds crunch and extra flavor while the spelt flour and oat bran lend an earthy flavor. This recipe can double as a morning coffee cake—imagine a rustic version of a carrot cake—if you bake the batter in a 9-inch round pan instead of individual muffin cups. Either way, top the batter with streusel before baking.

1. Preheat the oven to 350°F. Rub muffin tins with a ⅓-cup capacity with butter.

2. For the streusel topping, measure the flour, oat bran, sugars, and salt into a mixing bowl. Add the butter to the dry mixture. Rub the butter between your fingers, breaking it into smaller bits. Continue rubbing until the mixture feels coarse, like cornmeal. The more quickly you do this, the more the butter will stay solid, which is important for the success of the recipe.

3. Sift the dry ingredients into a large bowl, pouring back into the bowl any bits of grain and other ingredients that may remain in the sifter. Stir the carrots into the dry ingredients.

4. In a small bowl, whisk together the melted butter, buttermilk, and egg and whisk until thoroughly combined. Using a spatula, mix the wet ingredients into the dry ingredients and stir to combine.

5. Scoop the batter into 8 muffin cups, using a spoon or an ice cream scoop. The batter should be slightly mounded above the edge. Sprinkle the streusel topping evenly over the mounds of batter and press it into the batter slightly.

6. Bake for 32 to 35 minutes, rotating the pans halfway through. The muffins are ready to come out when they smell nutty and their bottoms are a dark golden-brown (twist a muffin out of the pan to check). Remove the tins from the oven, twist each muffin out, and place it on its side in the cup to cool. This ensures that the muffin stays crusty instead of getting soggy. These muffins are best eaten warm from the oven or later that same day. They can also be kept in an airtight container for up to 2 days, or frozen and reheated.

Note: To encourage even baking and to allow each muffin enough room to have an individual dome top, fill alternate cups in a 24-cup tin, or use two 12-cup tins.

Butter for the tins

STREUSEL TOPPING:

¼ cup plus 2 tablespoons spelt flour

2 tablespoons oat bran

2 tablespoons dark brown sugar

1 tablespoon sugar

⅛ teaspoon kosher salt

3 tablespoons cold unsalted butter, cut into ¼ inch pieces

DRY MIX:

1 cup spelt flour

¾ cup all-purpose flour

¼ cup oat bran

⅓ cup dark brown sugar

¼ cup sugar

1 teaspoon allspice

1 teaspoon kosher salt

1 teaspoon baking powder

½ teaspoon baking soda

½ teaspoon cinnamon

1½ cups coarsely grated carrots, about 2 medium

WET MIX:

2 ounces (½ stick) unsalted butter, melted and cooled slightly

1 cup buttermilk

1 egg

Huckle **Buckle**

STREUSEL TOPPING:

1/2 cup whole-grain pastry
   flour

1/2 cup spelt flour

3 tablespoons sugar

1 tablespoon dark brown
   sugar

1/2 teaspoon baking powder

1/2 teaspoon ground cinnamon

1/4 teaspoon kosher salt

3 tablespoons cold unsalted
   butter

1 egg

DRY MIX:

1 1/4 cups spelt flour

1 cup whole-grain pastry flour

1/2 cup dark brown sugar

1/2 cup sugar

1 tablespoon baking powder

1 teaspoon cinnamon

1 teaspoon kosher salt

4 ounces (1 stick) unsalted
   butter, softened

WET MIX:

3/4 cup whole milk

1/3 cup plain yogurt

4 egg yolks

2 teaspoons vanilla extract

2 cups blueberries or
   huckleberries

This is a morning coffee cake, made with a thick batter, two layers of berries, and a generous topping of streusel. As the cake bakes, the batter pushes up through the streusel, causing the cake to buckle—hence the "buckle" in its name. Although this recipe calls for blueberries, it's also delicious with more-difficult-to-find huckleberries—hence the "huckle" in the name. If you are using huckleberries, toss them in a little sugar first, as they're considerably more tart than blueberries. The batter can be made the night before and kept in the refrigerator overnight, ready to bake in the morning. The cake will need a few more minutes in the oven if it has been chilled overnight.

1. Preheat the oven to 350°F. Butter a 2 1/2-quart baking dish.
2. For the streusel topping, sift the flours, sugars, baking powder, cinnamon, and salt into a large bowl, pouring back into the bowl any bits of grain or other ingredients that may remain in the sifter. Cut the 3 tablespoons of cold butter into 1/4-inch pieces and add them to the dry mixture. Rub the butter between your fingers, breaking it into smaller bits. Continue rubbing until the mixture feels coarse, like cornmeal. The faster you do this, the better.
3. Whisk the egg thoroughly. Use a spatula to scrape the egg over the dry ingredients, then use your hands to mix the egg in. Squeeze handfuls of the dough together. The streusel topping should be in hazelnut-size clumps mixed with finer crumbs.
4. For the batter, place a sifter over the bowl of a standing mixer and sift the dry ingredients, pouring back into the bowl any bits of grain or other ingredients that may remain in the sifter. Add the softened butter to the bowl and attach the paddle. On medium speed, blend the butter into the flour mixture until combined.
5. In a large bowl, whisk together the milk, yogurt, egg yolks, and vanilla until thoroughly combined. Pour the milk mixture into the mixing bowl and paddle on low speed until the batter is smooth.
6. Scrape half the batter into the buttered dish. Sprinkle half of the berries over the surface. Scrape the remaining batter over the berries and gently spread it evenly in the pan. Sprinkle the last half of the blueberries over the batter and top with the streusel mixture.
7. Bake for 55 to 65 minutes, rotating the pan halfway through. The cake is done when it is golden brown and springs back when lightly touched, or when a skewer inserted in the center comes out clean. Allow the buckle to cool in the pan. It can be eaten warm, at room temperature, or cooled, wrapped tightly in plastic, and kept for up to 2 days.

Fig and Nut Muesli

Generous $1/4$ cup whole
   natural almonds
Generous $1/4$ cup pecan
   halves
Generous $1/4$ cup walnut
   halves
$1^{1}/2$ cups spelt flakes
$1/4$ cup plus 1 tablespoon
   flaxseed meal
$1/4$ cup quinoa flakes
2 tablespoons flaxseeds
Generous $1/2$ cup dried
   Black Mission figs
Generous $1/2$ cup dried
   Calimyrna figs
Generous $1/4$ cup dried
   apricots

FINISH:

Organic whole milk
Ripe seasonal fruit

Unlike more traditional Swiss muesli recipes, which often call for soaking oats in a cream mixture overnight and stirring fresh fruit over the top the next day, this muesli is definitely crunchy—although you can certainly soak a cup of this in milk or cream if you like. This recipe is loaded with dried fruit. Black Mission figs and the lighter and milder Calimyrna figs combine for a handsome two-toned color, while dried apricots lend tartness and a pretty touch of orange. The spelt flakes are toasted to give them an extra crunch, and so they no longer have a pasty flavor.

1. Place two racks at the upper and lower thirds of the oven and preheat to 350°F. Spread the almonds, pecans, and walnuts in a singe layer over a baking sheet. Toast in the oven until golden brown, 16 to 18 minutes, stirring the nuts halfway through.
2. While the nuts are toasting, spread the spelt flakes in a single layer on a baking sheet. Toast the spelt, simultaneously, until golden and crunchy, 6 to 8 minutes, stirring halfway through.
3. Remove both sheets from the oven and cool slightly. Once the nuts are cool enough to handle, chop them roughly into halves and in thirds and pour them into a large bowl. Add the toasted spelt flakes, $1/4$ cup flaxseed meal, quinoa flakes, and flaxseeds.
4. Pull the stems from all the figs and cut some in half and some in quarters. Mix the apricots with the remaining tablespoon of flaxseed meal (this keeps the apricots from sticking to your knife), and chop the apricots into smaller pieces. Toss the figs and the apricots into the nut-and-spelt mixture. Toss the muesli together with your hands.
5. To serve, scoop $1/2$ cup of muesli into a bowl and pour $1/2$ cup cold milk over the top, along with a generous handful of ripe seasonal fruit (wedges of juicy peaches, fresh berries, kiwi slices, or sweet pears). Add a sprinkle of salt and a drizzle of honey, if desired. The crunch of the nuts and the soft, ripe fruit are the stars of this bowl. The spelt should fall into the background.
6. If you won't be eating the muesli right away, wait until it's cooled completely and store it in an airtight container. It will keep for at least 2 weeks.

Ricotta **Crêpes**

These crêpes are a bit thicker than others, as they're made with the unusual addition of fresh ricotta. Be careful not to stir the ricotta too much, as the cheese creates little pockets in the batter that melt and toast as you cook the crêpes. Spelt flour adds flavor and a nuttiness that pairs well with the mild creaminess of the fresh cheese. Choose a ricotta made from whole milk without any thickening stabilizers. Heartier than many other crêpes, these are a terrific centerpiece for a meal. Serve them with wilted greens or some diced vine-ripened tomatoes.

1. In the order listed, measure all the ingredients except the ricotta into a blender jar or a narrow vessel with high sides that will accommodate an immersion blender. Blend the batter until it's smooth and free of clumps, cover, and leave to stand at room temperature for about 1 hour.

2. Use a spoon to stir the crêpe batter together to incorporate any of the liquid that may have separated. The batter should be the consistency of heavy cream. If it's thicker than that, stir in a few tablespoons of milk before adding the ricotta. Stir in the ricotta just until combined, taking care to leaves lumps of cheese flecked throughout. (Keep in mind that the batter will be stirred many more times during the griddling.)

3. Heat an 8-inch cast-iron or nonstick pan over medium high heat until a splash of water sizzles when it hits the pan. Rub the pan with butter. Hold the pan at an angle so that the handle is close to your body and tilted up, with the edge across from the handle tilted down toward the flame.

4. Using a 2-ounce ladle or ¼-cup measuring cup, scoop up some batter. Pour the batter just off-center in the pan and quickly swirl it around, aiming for one circular motion that creates a thin, even spread of batter in the pan. Do not add more batter to make up for empty space.

5. Cook the crêpe for about 1 minute, until the batter begins to bubble and the edges begin to brown. Slide a metal spatula or spoon along the edge to loosen the crêpe, pinch the edge, and flip the crêpe over in one motion. When the crêpe is flipped, the ricotta will create small mounds in the crêpe. Cook for another 45 seconds, or until the crêpes are speckled brown and crisp around the edges. Remove to a plate, with the pretty side facing up, and serve.

6. If you make the crêpes in advance, lay them individually on a baking sheet; before serving, toast them in a 400°F oven for 5 or 6 minutes until they are warm, tender in the middle, and crisp on the edges. They can also be warmed individually in a pan. Crêpes can also be frozen, wrapped tightly in plastic, with parchment between each crêpe .

Butter for the pan

1 cup whole milk, plus additional for thinning, if necessary

1 tablespoon honey

2 tablespoons unsalted butter, melted and cooled slightly

2 eggs

1 cup spelt flour

2 teaspoons kosher salt

FINISH:

1 cup fresh ricotta cheese

Olive Oil **Cake**

Olive oil for the pan

DRY MIX:

³/4 cup spelt flour

1¹/2 cups all-purpose flour

³/4 cup sugar

1¹/2 teaspoons baking
   powder

³/4 teaspoon kosher salt

WET MIX:

3 eggs

1 cup olive oil

³/4 cup whole milk

1¹/2 tablespoons fresh
   rosemary, finely chopped

5 ounces bittersweet
   chocolate (about 70
   percent cacao), cut into
   roughly ¹/2-inch pieces

If you have yet to try your hand at baking an olive oil cake, you might be a bit hesitant, thinking it might be too—well, oily, or questioning the wisdom of pouring pricy olive oil into a cake batter. But this olive oil cake is amazing. It has a fine crumb from the spelt flour, and the unlikely combination of rosemary and chocolate bring out the spice and fruitiness of the olive oil. And since you're substituting oil for butter, it's neither greasy nor particularly more expensive. You don't need to use a specialty olive oil for this cake, but if you have one that has a lot of flavor, the cake will be that much better.

1. Position a rack in the middle of the oven and preheat to 350°F. Rub a 9¹/2-inch fluted tart pan with olive oil.
2. Sift the dry ingredients into a large bowl, pouring back into the bowl any bits of grain or other ingredients that may remain in the sifter, and set aside.
3. In a large bowl, whisk the eggs thoroughly. Add the olive oil, milk, and rosemary and whisk again. Using a spatula, fold the wet ingredients into the dry ingredients, gently mixing just until combined. Stir in the chocolate. Pour the batter into the pan, spreading it evenly and smoothing the top.
4. Bake for about 40 minutes, or until the top is domed, golden brown, and darker around the edges, and a skewer inserted into the center comes out clean. The cake can be eaten warm or cool from the pan, or cooled, wrapped tightly in plastic, and kept for up to 2 days.

Focaccia

Olive oil for the bowl and
   pans

1 package active dry yeast
Pinch of sugar

1$^{1}/_{2}$ cups spelt flour
1$^{1}/_{2}$ cups all-purpose flour,
   plus additional for
   kneading
1 tablespoon kosher salt
$^{1}/_{4}$ cup plus 2 tablespoons
   olive oil
Herbs, spices, or other
   toppings of choice

Focaccia dough is a moist dough that only gets better with age. Stored in the refrigerator, the dough develops a more complex flavor, and you can pull part or all of it out to make dinner—just be sure it has time to come to room temperature before shaping. You can top the focaccia with almost anything: a liberal pour of olive oil and a dusting of salt, a handful of fresh herbs, olives or sautéed vegetables and cheese, or a meaty tomato sauce. However you plan to top your focaccia, before cooking pour a generous glug of olive oil over the top—especially around the edges—for a crunchy golden crust.

1. Lightly rub a large bowl with olive oil. Add 1$^{1}/_{4}$ cups of warm water, the yeast, and sugar to another large bowl. Stir, and allow the yeast to bloom for about 5 minutes, until it begins to bubble. (If it doesn't, it may be inactive; throw it out and start over with a new package.)

2. Add the flours, salt, and 2 tablespoons olive oil to the yeast mixture and stir to combine. Pour the dough onto a lightly floured surface and begin to knead together, adding up to $^{1}/_{2}$ cup of all-purpose flour to the dough as necessary to keep it from sticking. Knead the dough for about 10 minutes, or until it is supple and elastic.

3. For the first rise, put the dough into the oiled bowl, turning it so that the top of the dough is coated with oil. Cover with a towel and leave for about 2 hours, or until doubled in size (see Sidebar, page 130).

4. Generously oil a baking sheet or 3 9-inch round pans with olive oil.

5. For the second rise, place the dough on the baking sheet or divide the dough into 3 pieces and put 1 piece in each of the oiled pans. Stretch the dough out with your hands so that it covers the surface of the baking sheet or pans, and dimple it with your fingers. Cover with a towel or plastic wrap and leave to rise for 1 hour.

6. Position two racks in the upper and lower thirds of the oven (or put a single rack in the middle if you're using one baking sheet) and preheat to 400°F.

7. After the dough has completed its second rise and has puffed up on the sheet or in the pans, top it with $^{1}/_{4}$ cup of olive oil and sprinkle it with salt, herbs or spices, or the toppings of your choice.

8. Bake for 22 to 25 minutes, until golden brown. Allow the bread to cool slightly in the pan before slicing and serving. Focaccia is best eaten the day it's made.

9. If you wish to store the focaccia dough for future use, after the first rise is complete, wrap the dough tightly in plastic and store in the refrigerator for up to 5 days. Pull all or part of the dough out when you wish to use it; bring to room temperature before shaping the dough and continuing with the recipe.

Chocolate Chocolate **Cookies**

In some baked goods, you just need a lot of sugar. Sugar not only provides sweetness; it's also what gives a cookie its crust and crumb. In this recipe, sugar produces a crackly surface and wonderfully chewy edges. The sweetness of the sugar is offset by dark, bittersweet chocolate and cacao nibs, which are crunchy, roasted cocoa beans that have been separated from their husks and broken into small pieces. They're somewhat like mildly roasted coffee beans, but with a definite chocolate flavor—they add a nubby texture and a slight bite to the cookies. When you're making this recipe, keep in mind that the cookies will need to chill for two hours before they are baked. Use good-quality chocolate, as it makes all the difference.

1. Melt the butter and chocolate in a double boiler or in the microwave, stirring until combined and thoroughly melted.
2. Add the eggs and the sugar to the bowl of a standing mixer fitted with a whisk attachment. Immediately turn the mixer to high speed and whip for 3 minutes. Using a spatula, scrape every bit of the warm chocolate mixture into the mixing bowl. Mix on low speed to combine.
3. Sift the dry ingredients into a large bowl, pouring back into the bowl any bits of grain or other ingredients that may remain in the sifter. Add the dry ingredients to the chocolate mixture and mix on low speed until combined. Remove the bowl from the mixer and scrape down the sides and the bottom of the bowl. Add the remaining chopped chocolate and stir until evenly combined. Chill for at least 2 hours or up to 3 days.
4. Place two racks in the upper and lower thirds of the oven and preheat to 350°F. Line two baking sheets with parchment.

Although you can butter the sheets instead, parchment is very useful for these cookies because the large chunks of chocolate tend to stick to the pan.

5. Scoop balls of dough about 2 tablespoons in size. Roll the balls in cacao nibs, covering all but the bottom of the dough with the nibs. Place the balls onto the baking sheets, leaving about 3 inches between them, or about 6 to a sheet.
6. Bake the cookies for 17 to 20 minutes, rotating the sheets halfway through. The cookies will still be soft in the centers but the edges will feel firm and the cacao nibs will be toasted a dark brown. Transfer the cookies, still on the parchment, to the counter to cool. Reline the baking sheets with parchment and repeat with the remaining dough. These cookies are best eaten warm from the oven or later that same day. They'll keep in an airtight container for up to 3 days.

Parchment for the
   baking sheets

WET MIX:

8 ounces (2 sticks) unsalted
   butter
8 ounces bittersweet
   chocolate (about 70
   percent cacao), coarsely
   chopped
4 eggs
2 1/4 cups sugar

DRY MIX:

2 cups spelt flour
1 tablespoon plus 1 teaspoon
   baking powder
2 teaspoons kosher salt

8 ounces bittersweet
   chocolate (70 to 75%
   cacao), coarsely chopped

FINISH:

1 cup cacao nibs

teff

Unless you frequent Ethiopian restaurants, you've probably never heard of teff, let alone eaten anything made with flour ground from this tiny grain. Teff flour is fine and grainy, with a malty aroma and a pale cocoa color. This distinctive maltiness makes teff flour a great match for nuts and dried fruit. It is a particularly fine flour, so pairing it with wheat flours gives me the crumb that I look for in my recipes.

An obvious starting place for experimenting with teff was *injera*. These are traditional Ethiopian flatbreads, similar to crêpes, that are used as both plates and utensils, with bits torn off the edges as the whole dish is eaten by hand. Since teff does not have any gluten, teff flour is mixed with whole-wheat flour into a starter and fermented overnight, sometimes a day or two longer. This brief fermentation gives *injera* their distinctly sour taste.

You can use teff flour for a lot more than *injera*, although it needs to be paired with other flours to mellow its flavor and lend structure to a recipe. Adding all-purpose flour or whole-wheat flour to a percentage of teff flour can accomplish both of these things; in fact, many of the *injera* made outside of Ethiopia and Eritrea are made with a blend of flours. Teff flour often works best when used in smaller proportion to a wheat flour, without sacrificing any of its distinctive qualities. In the Grahams, teff flour is the key to the crackers' crispness and rich mahogany color. The Hazelnut Muffins were a challenge to get right, but once I added teff flour, muffins that were once oily and coarse became tender and soft, and the roasted hazelnuts met their match.

In the Date Nut Bread, a purée of Medjool dates is stirred into a batter made with teff and all-purpose flour, lending sweetness as well as a smooth consistency that offsets the grainy nature of the flour. Teff flour helps lighten the crumb, keeping the cake from getting too dense.

When experimenting with teff flour, I also found that brown butter—butter that has been cooked down until the milk solids separate and caramelize—has a fantastic affinity for the flour. The cooked butter, with its dark flecks and wonderfully nutty taste, adds richness and depth to the teff flour. In fact, I liked this combination so much that I put it into two of the recipes in this chapter: the Hazelnut Muffins mentioned above and the Brown Butter Scones.

Injera

1 teaspoon active dry yeast
   (about ¹/₂ package)
¹/₂ cup teff flour
1 cup whole-wheat flour
¹/₂ teaspoon kosher salt

***Injera*, traditional Ethiopian flatbreads made with teff** flour, are large and thin, like spongy pancakes. The *injera* in this recipe are cooked more like European crêpes, on both sides rather than just one. This batter rests overnight to develop the characteristic acidic flavor, but it could rest for as long as three days, depending on how sour you prefer your bread. Make a stack of *injera* for dinner and roll them up around cheese and greens or charred peppers. You can forgo utensils entirely (*injera* is traditionally a plate, fork, and spoon), tear off bits of *injera*, and use them to scoop up stews or sauces.

1. Measure the yeast into a large bowl. Heat 2 cups water in a small saucepan over low heat to a temperature that is warm to the touch, about 100°F, and pour it over the yeast. Stir together to combine. Add the flours and the salt and stir again. Cover the bowl with a towel or plastic wrap and let it sit on the counter overnight.

2. The next evening, whisk the mixture until smooth.

3. Griddling *injera* is just like griddling a crêpe. Heat an 8-inch cast-iron or nonstick pan over a high flame until a splash of water sizzles when it hits the pan. Rub the pan with butter. Hold the pan at an angle so that the handle is close to your body and tilted up, with the edge across from the handle tilted down toward the flame.

4. Using a 2-ounce ladle or ¹/₄-cup measuring cup, scoop up some batter. Pour the batter just off-center in the pan and quickly swirl it around, aiming for one circular motion that creates a thin, even spread of batter in the pan. Do not add more batter to make up for empty space.

5. Cook the *injera* for about 1 minute, until the batter begins to bubble, leaving pinprick holes on the surface, and the edges begin to brown. Slide a metal spatula or spoon along the edge to loosen the *injera*, pinch the edge of the *injera*, and flip the *injera* over in one motion. Cook for 45 seconds longer, or until speckled brown and crisp around the edges. Remove to a plate, with the pretty side facing up. As you continue to cook the *injera*, you may need to adjust the heat, turning it up or down to keep results consistent.

6. If the *injera* are made in advance, lay them individually on a baking sheet to toast in a 400°F oven for 5 or 6 minutes before serving, until they are warm, tender in the middle, and crisp on the edges. The *injera* can also be warmed individually in a pan. *Injera* can also be frozen, wrapped tightly in plastic, with parchment separating each one.

Hazelnut **Muffins**

Teff flour, with its deep brown color and distinctly malty flavor, is a fantastic match for the richness of hazelnuts. In this recipe, the unpeeled nuts are toasted in browning butter. Keeping the skins on is not only easier, but it also adds an earthy taste and delicate flecks of dark brown to the crumb. Browning the butter in the pan with the nuts infuses the butter, and thus the muffins, with the flavor of the hazelnuts. These muffins are topped with a sprinkling of finely chopped hazelnuts and spiced sugar before they're baked.

1. Preheat the oven to 350°F. Rub muffin tins with a 1/3-cup capacity with butter.
2. Place the butter, hazelnuts, and salt in a small heavy-bottomed pan and cook over medium heat, swirling the pan occasionally and watching for the edges of the nuts to turn golden brown. Remove the pan from the flame before the nuts get too brown, as they will continue to cook in the hot butter. Pour them into a bowl to cool down.
3. In a small bowl, stir together the finely chopped hazelnuts, sugar, nutmeg, and cinnamon. Set aside.
4. Sift the dry ingredients into a large bowl, pouring back into the bowl any flour or other ingredients that may remain in the sifter.
5. In a medium bowl, whisk the wet ingredients until thoroughly combined.
6. Pour the hazelnut butter over the dry ingredients, and then the buttermilk mixture over the top of that. Using a spatula, mix together the wet and dry ingredients.
7. Scoop the batter into 10 muffin cups, using a spoon or an ice cream scoop. The batter should be mounded above the edges of the cups. Sprinkle the hazelnut topping evenly over the batter, gently pressing it into the batter so that it adheres.
8. Bake for 22 to 26 minutes, rotating the pans halfway through. The muffins are ready to come out when they smell nutty, the hazelnuts are toasted, and the bottoms are golden in color (twist a muffin out of the pan to check). Remove the tins from the oven, twist each muffin out, and place it on its side in the cup to cool. This ensures that the muffin stays crusty instead of getting soggy. These muffins are best eaten warm from the oven. They can also be kept in an airtight container for up to 2 days.

Butter for the tins

4 ounces (1 stick) unsalted butter
1/2 cup raw hazelnuts, skins on, chopped into rough halves
1/2 teaspoon kosher salt

FINISH:

1/2 cup raw hazelnuts, skins on, finely chopped
1/4 cup sugar
1 teaspoon nutmeg, freshly grated
1/2 teaspoon cinnamon

DRY MIX:

1 cup whole-wheat flour
3/4 cup teff flour
1/2 cup all-purpose flour
1/2 cup sugar
1 tablespoon baking powder
1/2 teaspoon baking soda
1 teaspoon kosher salt

WET MIX:

1 cup buttermilk
1/2 cup plain yogurt
2 eggs
1 teaspoon pure vanilla extract

Note: To encourage even baking and to allow each muffin enough room to have an individual dome top, fill alternate cups in a 24-cup tin, or use two 12-cup tins.

Grahams

Butter for the baking sheets

DRY MIX:

1 cup graham flour

¹/₂ cup teff flour

³/₄ cup all-purpose flour

¹/₂ cup dark brown sugar

1 teaspoon baking soda

1 teaspoon kosher salt

¹/₈ teaspoon cinnamon

¹/₈ teaspoon ground allspice

¹/₈ teaspoon ground cloves

WET MIX:

3 ounces (³/₄ stick) unsalted
    butter, melted and cooled
    slightly

¹/₄ cup honey

1 tablespoon unsulphured
    (not blackstrap) molasses

¹/₃ cup whole milk

FINISH:

¹/₄ cup sugar

¹/₂ teaspoon cinnamon

Nothing gets a four-year-old's attention quite as quickly as the mention of graham crackers, or "grahams," as they're called at my daughter's nursery school. Named after Reverend Sylvester Graham, the man who first championed graham flour, these cookies are made with a blend of graham flour (coarsely ground whole wheat), teff flour, and all-purpose flour, for just the right crispness. Most of the sweetness comes from honey and brown sugar, a tablespoon of molasses lending a slightly bitter edge. I like cutting these cookies into the traditional rectangles, but you can use any shape or size that you want. Don't forget the tiny holes!

1. Sift the dry ingredients into a large bowl, pouring back any bits of flour or other ingredients that may remain in the sifter.

2. In a medium bowl, whisk together the melted butter, honey, molasses, and milk.

3. Pour the wet ingredients over the dry ingredients. Stir the ingredients into a moist cookie dough. Press the dough into a disk, wrap in plastic, and chill for a minimum of 1 hour or up to 3 days.

4. Preheat the oven to 350°F. Rub two baking sheets lightly with butter.

5. Dust a work surface with flour. Remove the dough from the refrigerator and divide it in half, working with one half while keeping the other half chilled. Use your hands to flatten the first half until it is ¹/₂ inch thick.

6. Dust the counter and both sides of the dough with flour. With a rolling pin, roll out the dough until it's ¹/₈-inch thick. Move the dough around frequently to make sure it isn't sticking. If it is, slide a pastry scraper under the dough and dust the counter or the dough with flour.

7. Use a sharp floured knife to cut the dough into 5-by-2¹/₂-inch rectangles and transfer the shapes onto the baking sheets. Cut these rectangles into the traditional quarters, without seperating them—this keeps the lines showing even after baking. Using a fork or a skewer, press holes into the surface of the cookies.

8. Stir the sugar and cinnamon together and sprinkle each cookie with a few pinches of the mixture.

9. Bake for 15 to 17 minutes, rotating the pans halfway through. The grahams are ready when the edge is a darker shade of brown than the rest of the cookie. Remove from the oven and allow to cool on a rack so the grahams become crisp. If the cookies are not quite crisp enough, next time they either need to bake longer or be rolled out thinner.

10. Repeat with the remaining half of the dough.

11. These cookies are best eaten once cooled. They'll keep in an airtight container for up to 3 days.

Date Nut **Bread**

Butter for the pan

1½ cups pecan halves

2 teaspoons olive oil

½ teaspoon kosher salt

8 large Medjool dates, halved
   and pitted

DRY MIX:

1 cup all-purpose flour

1 cup whole-grain pastry
   flour

½ cup teff flour

1 tablespoon baking powder

2 teaspoons nutmeg, freshly
   grated

1 teaspoon kosher salt

WET MIX:

4 ounces (1 stick) cold
   unsalted butter

⅓ cup sugar

2 eggs

⅓ cup honey

½ cup plain yogurt

Loaded with dates and toasted pecans, this is a deeply satisfying quick bread. The dates are soaked in warm water to soften, then puréed to make a thick fruit butter. This purée, along with the yogurt, is what gives the cake its moistness. Slather a slice with butter or serve it with a plate of after-dinner cheeses.

1. Preheat the oven to 350°F. Toss the pecans in the oil and salt and spread the nuts evenly on a baking sheet. Toast the pecans in the middle of the oven until golden brown, 12 to 15 minutes. Set the pecans aside to cool, but keep the oven heated.

2. Meanwhile, bring ½ cup water to a boil and pour over the dates. Let the dates soften while you prepare the remaining ingredients.

3. Rub a standard loaf pan lightly with butter.

4. Sift the dry ingredients into a large bowl, pouring back into the bowl any bits of grains or other ingredients that may remain in the sifter, and set aside.

5. Put the butter and sugar into the bowl of a standing mixer fitted with a paddle attachment. Turn the mixer to medium speed and cream until light in color, about 3 minutes.

6. Meanwhile, using an immersion blender or a food processor, blend the dates with the soaking water until smooth. Scrape the date purée into a medium bowl. Add the eggs, honey, and yogurt to the date purée and whisk until thoroughly combined.

7. Pour half of the date mixture into the bowl of the mixer and mix on low speed until combined. Add half of the dry ingredients and mix until just combined. Pour the remaining date mixture into the bowl, then the remaining flour, and mix on high speed for 1 minute. Remove the bowl from the mixer and scrape down the sides and the bottom of the bowl to incorporate all of the ingredients. Add the pecans and stir them throughout the batter.

8. Scrape the batter into the loaf pan and smooth out the top.

9. Bake on the middle rack of the oven for 70 to 75 minutes, rotating the pan halfway through. When it is ready, the bread will smell like it is on the brink of burning; it should be deeply brown and even darker along the edges; and a skewer inserted in the center should come out clean.

10. As soon as you remove the bread from the oven, flip it out of the pan; then flip it right side up and transfer it to a cooling rack. Let the loaf cool thoroughly before you slice into it. It can be kept, tightly wrapped, for 3 days.

Brown Butter **Scones**

MAKES 8

Brown butter is true kitchen alchemy. Watch a stick of butter melt in a pan, transforming from frothy yellow to brilliant gold to a rich, dark brown in a matter of minutes. As the milk solids caramelize, the butter clarifies, and a gorgeous aroma overtakes your kitchen while the butter browns into a golden sauce that tastes almost like hazelnuts. Teff flour and brown butter are a natural pairing; with their dark brown shades and nutty flavors, they enhance each other beautifully.

1. Melt the butter in a high-sided saucepan over medium heat. Swirl the pan to encourage even melting. At first the butter will melt to gold, followed by white foam that begins bubbling around the edges and moves toward the center—it sounds almost like popcorn popping as the butter pops and sizzles in the pan. Next, the butter solids form a bubbling raft. You may be tempted to stop here. Don't. The butter will rise up the sides of the pan and small brown flecks will dot the surface. Give the pan a swirl and continue cooking until the bottom of the pan is covered in dark brown flecks and your kitchen smells toasty. If the butter is about to overflow, stick a metal whisk into it and it will descend.

2. Pour the brown butter into a wide, shallow container, scraping all of the dark flecks at the bottom of the pan into the container (that color is flavor), and freeze until solid. The larger the surface area of the container, the faster the butter will freeze. This step can be done a day or more ahead of time.

3. While the butter is freezing, preheat the oven to 350°F. Rub a baking sheet with butter.

4. Measure the dry ingredients into the bowl of a food processor. Once the butter has frozen solid, cut it into pieces and add them to the dry ingredients. Pulse until the butter is ground to meal, about 20 seconds. Pour the butter-flour mixture into a large bowl.

5. In a small bowl, whisk the cream, egg, and vanilla until thoroughly combined. Add the wet ingredients to the dry ingredients and stir gently to combine.

6. Turn the dough out onto a lightly floured work surface and fold together a few times to form a cohesive ball. Flatten the dough into a disk about 1 inch thick and 7 inches wide, taking care to soften the edges with your hands to keep them from cracking. Cut the disk into 8 wedges.

7. Place the wedges onto the baking sheet, making sure that they're at least a few inches apart. Brush the tops of the scones very lightly with cream, twice. Then sprinkle the scones with sugar.

8. Bake for 28 to 34 minutes, until the scones are browning around the edges and on the top. These scones are best baked darker rather than lighter.

Butter for the baking sheet

4 ounces (1 stick) unsalted butter

DRY MIX:
$1/2$ cup teff flour
1 cup all-purpose flour
1 cup whole rolled oats
$1/4$ cup dark brown sugar
$1/4$ cup sugar
2 teaspoons baking powder
$1 1/4$ teaspoons kosher salt

WET MIX:
$1/2$ cup heavy cream
1 egg
1 teaspoon pure vanilla extract

FINISH:
Heavy cream, for brushing
Sugar, granulated or turbinado

jams and compotes

Every summer, I am the person who arrives at the farmers' market with a wagon meant for carrying my kids and invariably leaves with the wagon filled with cases of fruit, while my kids walk alongside helping me pull it. I can't resist the dappled skin of a sun-ripened peach, or those small, juicy strawberries, or the faintly dusty apples right off the trees that crunch when you eat them, or the blush of a ripe apricot. I love fruit—and the farmers that grow it. If you have a local farmers' market, I absolutely recommend buying your fruit there. The flavor is so much better than you can find in any store.

Naturally, fruits have found their way into many of the recipes in this book, since they go so well with all the pure, nutty, earthy flavors of whole-grain flours. I decided to devote an entire chapter to fruit jams and compotes rather than bury them among the flour recipes. Fruit is

Naturally, **fruits have found** their way into many of the **recipes in this book**, since they **go so well** with all the **pure**, nutty, earthy **flavors of** whole-grain flours.

meant to be eaten seasonally, and the fruits in this chapter represent all four seasons. That way, if you make the Strawberry Barley Scones in the middle of winter, try the Fig Butter instead. Or, in the summer, top the Quinoa Porridge with a dollop of Apricot Jam instead of Squash and Apple Compote.

With the right fruit, you'll find that cooking is simple and straightforward. Basically all you need to make jams and compotes is fruit and sugar—butter, spices, and herbs are all optional. Choosing flavorful fruit means that you'll only need to use a small amount of sugar. Choose fruits with some tartness—taste them—to balance out the sugar in the recipe.

For making jam, choose a wide, deep pot, preferably the biggest one you have in your kitchen. A wide surface area allows steam to escape quickly, resulting in a shorter cooking time and a brighter-tasting jam. A proper jam-making pot should have a heavy bottom to prevent scorching and high sides to protect your arms from any splattering sugar. A Dutch oven or enameled cast-iron casserole is perfect. Don't use an aluminum pot, as the metal reacts badly and can leach into your jam.

At the beginning of the cooking process, you'll need to coax the moisture out of the fruit. Sometimes this happens over low heat, sometimes over high. The method depends on the fruit and the recipe. Extracting the water from the fruit provides enough liquid for you to cook the jam to the right consistency without scorching it or having to add juice or additional water. Juice can cloud jams, and while you can add water (and sometimes need to, as in the Three-Citrus Marmalade), you'll prefer the natural, more flavorful moisture from the fruit itself.

Bringing the fruit to a quick simmer and rapidly cooking it keeps the jam tasting fresh. Stir quickly and continuously to release the steam and thicken the jam. Keep the heat as high as you can stand it (the higher it is, the more the jam will splatter, but steady stirring keeps this at a minimum). A medium-high heat is usually best, but as the jam nears completion, you may need to turn it down a little.

Cooking with fruit requires that you use **all of your senses**.

Listen carefully to the **sounds in the pan**.

Cooking with fruit requires that you use all of your senses. Listen carefully to the sounds in the pan. Do you hear sizzling, rapid bubbling, or slow, gentle popping noises? Watch for the size of the bubbles as they change in the pan. The jam is nearly ready when you can begin to hear and feel the scraping of the spoon on the bottom of the pan. These are all clues to tell you what is going on in the pan. Caramelizing and sautéing fruit for compotes requires similar attention to detail.

When you're cooking fruit at the stove, slow down; really take the time to watch the transformation happening in the pan. Practice offers the clues you need to do it right. And always remember that the finished jam, compote, or fruit butter is the direct result of the fruit that you started with.

Apricot Jam

3 pounds apricots
1/2 to 3/4 cup sugar,
   depending on how sweet
   you like your jam

This recipe is about as simple as it gets—a spoonable preserve made with just fresh apricots and a bit of sugar. My favorite apricots are Blenheims, which are small, dappled, and very orange, with just a bit of green where they've been pulled from the tree. When perfectly ripe, Blenheims give when gently squeezed, and you can find a small puddle of juice at the pit. If you don't have access to Blenheims, chose floral and flavorful apricots.

1. Put a small plate into the freezer for testing the jam later. Set up an ice bath by filling a large bowl with ice and about 1 cup of water. Set a smaller bowl on the counter next to it. (Do not set the smaller bowl inside the larger bowl yet; if you do, condensation will line the bowl and water down your jam.) Put a rubber spatula next to the bowls.

2. Split the apricots in half and remove the pits. Add the apricots and the sugar to a 5- to 7-quart pot. Give the fruit a stir with a sturdy wooden spoon. Set the pot over a medium flame and cook for about 5 minutes, stirring occasionally, until the apricots have softened and the sugar has melted.

3. Turn the heat up to medium-high and cook for 15 to 20 minutes, stirring the fruit constantly. As the apricots warm up, their juices begin to run, leaving the halves of apricots surrounded by their nectar. After a few moments more, the apricots should transform into a soft orange purée with steam wafting up from the pot. Finally, the jam should thicken slightly into a combination of purée and intact pieces of fruit.

4. Near the end of the cooking time, clip a candy thermometer to the side of the pot. The finished temperature of this jam should hover at about 200°F. When the jam is done, move the pot to a cool burner. (Don't leave it on the burner it has cooked on; even if you turn the flame off, the residual heat will overcook the jam.)

5. Remove the plate from the freezer. Test the jam by placing a spoonful of it on the plate (see Sidebar, page 190). It should thicken promptly when you do so.

6. When the jam is finished, using potholders, pour the pot of jam into the smaller bowl. Scrape out every bit with the spatula. Set the bowl into the ice bath and stir the jam a few times to allow some of the heat to escape.

7. Cover the jam with plastic wrap so that the plastic is touching the surface of the jam, to keep a skin from forming. Once the jam is completely cooled, it can be stored in the refrigerator for up to 2 weeks.

Onion **Jam**

I'm always surprised by caramelized onions, a rich jam made by simply cooking down slices of this kitchen staple. How can something so humble become so rich in flavor? As the onions cook, they condense from their pungent raw state to a thick, sweet spread. Don't be alarmed at the volume of raw onions in your pot—as they cook, they reduce to a remarkably small amount of jam. If you have a big pot, you may even want to double the recipe.

2 pounds yellow onions,
    about 7 1/2 cups sliced
1 tablespoon olive oil
1 teaspoon kosher salt
1/2 teaspoon freshly ground
    black pepper, or to taste
1 teaspoon red wine vinegar

1. Cut the stem ends off the onions. Slice each onion in half through the root end. Lay each onion half cut side down and slice it, toward the root, into slices about 1/4 inch thick.

2. Heat a 5- to 7-quart heavy-bottomed pot over a medium-high flame. Add the olive oil and heat until it's shimmering. Add the onions, salt, and pepper and stir to coat the onions with the oil. Sauté the onions for 10 to 15 minutes, stirring occasionally, until the onions have lost their gloss, the bottom of the pan is getting dark in areas, and the edges of the onions are beginning to brown. Turn the flame to low, cover the pot, and cook for 20 minutes.

3. Uncover the pan, stir the onions, scrape any dark flavorful bits from the bottom of the pan, and continue to cook, uncovered, for 1 hour more. Stir the onions occasionally, especially towards the end of the cooking time, to prevent burning. The onions are ready when the liquid has evaporated and the onions are dark, translucent, and jammy. Stir in the vinegar and allow to cool. The onion jam will keep in the refrigerator for 2 weeks, or in the freezer for 1 month.

Strawberry Jam

MAKES ABOUT 4 CUPS

3 pounds strawberries

1 cup sugar

OPTIONAL FLAVORINGS:

Zest of 2 organic limes

1 tablespoon high-quality
   balsamic vinegar

12 organic lavender stems

12 sprigs of organic oregano

Making strawberry jam is a spring ritual in my kitchen, especially at the peak of the season when the berries are at the height of their flavor. In this recipe, strawberries are cooked in a boiling sugar syrup, giving the finished jam both gloss and thickness without extra sweetness. Cooking the jam over high heat is the key to its fresh flavor. Once the jam is off the heat, you'll have a classic strawberry jam, simple and straightforward. If you want to add an interesting layer of flavor to the berries, I've listed four flavoring options: a bright, tart lime; balsamic vinegar, meaty and rich; herbaceous fresh oregano; and a floral lavender.

1. Put a small plate into the freezer for testing the jam later. Set up an ice bath by filling a large bowl with ice and about 1 cup water. Set a smaller bowl on the counter next to it. (Do not set the smaller bowl inside the larger bowl yet; if you do, condensation will line the bowl and water down your jam.) Put a rubber spatula next to the bowls.

2. Hull the strawberries, cutting larger berries in half and leaving smaller berries whole.

3. Measure ½ cup water and the sugar into a heavy-bottomed 5- to 7-quart pot. Let the mixture sit for a minute to combine.

4. Bring the sugar mixture to a boil over a high flame and cook, without stirring, until the syrup is gently bubbling all across the surface, 5 to 7 minutes. At first the bubbles will be small, boiling rapidly, and clustering around the edges; when the syrup is nearly ready, the bubbles will be about the size of quarters, bubbling slowly and evenly across the surface. The syrup shouldn't caramelize; if any color begins to form, swirl the pan and add the fruit immediately.

5. Add the strawberries and stir with a wooden spoon or heatproof spatula. With the heat on medium-high, cook the berries for 15 to 20 minutes, stirring constantly, until the syrup thickens to a jammy consistency; some of the berries will have broken down and some will still have their shape.

6. When the jam is nearly ready, clip a candy thermometer to the side of the pot. The

The Frozen-Plate Test

This is a method I use to test the thickness of a jam or marmalade. Scoop a small spoonful of cooked jam onto a plate that has been chilled in the freezer. This cools down the jam instantly and allows you to see if it's the right consistency. Does it keep its shape? Does liquid puddle around the edge of the mound? Run your finger through it and see if a trail remains. Hold the plate up at an angle and see how far and how quickly the jam runs down the plate. In my jam making, I look for a mound of jam that keeps its shape on the plate, without a puddle of liquid, and with a soft trail. When the plate is held up, the jam should move slowly down the surface. Of course, the consistency of your jam depends on your preference—you may like it slightly thicker or looser.

190   GOOD TO THE GRAIN

temperature of the finished jam should be about 210°F. When the jam is done, move the pot to a cool burner. (Don't leave it on the burner it has cooked on; even if you turn the flame off, the residual heat will overcook the jam.)

7. Remove the plate from the freezer. Test the jam by placing a spoonful of it on the plate (see Sidebar). It should thicken promptly when you do so.

8. When the jam is finished, using potholders, pour the pot of jam into the smaller bowl. Scrape out every bit with the spatula. Set the bowl into the ice bath and stir the jam a few times to allow some of the heat to escape.

9. You now have a classic strawberry jam. If you want to add some extra flavor, at this point you can infuse the jam with herbs, spices, or other ingredients. Finely zest the limes over the bowl of warm jam, so that the jam captures the lime oil as well as the zest. Or stir in balsamic vinegar. Or hold sprigs of oregano or lavender in your hand like a bouquet and stir them around the jam. Do about 10 slow stirs—stirring for longer than a minute will infuse too much flavor. Remove the sprigs from the jam, wiping off any excess jam as you pull them out.

10. Cover the jam with plastic wrap so that the plastic is touching the surface of the jam, to keep a skin from forming. Once the jam is completely cooled, it can be stored in the refrigerator for 2 weeks.

Three-Citrus **Marmalade**

5 organic oranges

4 organic blood oranges

4 organic Meyer lemons,
   or substitute 2 organic
   oranges and 2 organic
   lemons

3 cups sugar

Marmalade recipes have always seemed like too much work to me—you have to peel and chop the fruit, bag seeds and pith for pectin, rest things overnight, then boil and measure hot liquid to determine how much sugar to put in. So when it came time for me to develop a marmalade of my own, I streamlined as many of the steps as I could. Marmalade is different from other jams, in that there isn't much stirring necessary until the end. Until the last twenty minutes, the syrup more or less reduces on its own. This recipe uses three kinds of citrus fruits that are Southern California favorites—but there's plenty of room for substitution if you have others in your markets, or in your back yard.

1. Put a small plate into the freezer for testing the jam later. Set up an ice bath by filling a large bowl with ice and about 1 cup of water. Set a smaller bowl on the counter next to it. (Do not set the smaller bowl inside the larger bowl yet; if you do, condensation will line the bowl and water down your jam.) Put a rubber spatula next to the bowls.

2. Scrub and dry the citrus. With a vegetable peeler, strip the zest (the outermost layer of the rind) from 1 orange, 2 blood oranges, and 2 Meyer lemons. Slice the strips into thin matchsticks about $1/16$ inch in width. Keep any irregular shapes—don't worry if the slices are uneven. Add the strips to a small pot and cover with cold water. Over high heat, bring the pot to a boil and boil for 30 seconds. Drain the strips, rinse with cold water, and set aside.

3. Cut off both ends of each fruit. Using the side of your knife, go around each fruit from top to bottom, removing both the pith and the peel. The thoroughness with which you clean your fruit will show in the final product, so remove as much of the white pith as you can. Discard the peels, or compost them if you can. Cut the fruit into quarters, picking out the seeds and removing the harder, pithy centers. Chop each fruit into roughly 1- to 2-inch pieces, saving all of the juice that drips onto the cutting board.

4. Measure the fruit (you should have about 6 cups) and any remaining juice into a 5- to 7-quart heavy-bottomed pot. Add 6 cups water (filtered, if you have it) to the pot with the fruit and bring the mixture to a boil over high heat.

5. When the mixture has come to a boil, lower the flame to medium. Cook the fruit syrup, uncovered, for about 1 hour, or until it has reduced by half (a piece of masking tape stuck to the outside of the pot is a good indicator of your starting point, although you can usually see a cooking line inside the pot). For a clear marmalade, periodically skim off any white scum that accumulates at the top, and stir occasionally over the course of the hour.

6. Add the blanched zest and the sugar to the pot. Stir to combine, increase the heat to high, and bring the mixture to a boil. Reduce the heat to medium and cook, about 10 minutes. The mixture should be at a bubbling simmer; adjust the heat upward if it's not. After 10 minutes, begin to stir the marmalade constantly, adjusting the heat if necessary so that it stays at a rapid simmer; the zest is now candying and the marmalade thickening. Cook for 20 minutes more.

7. The marmalade is ready when it is thick enough that a spoon makes a scraping sound and leaves a trail at the bottom of the pan.

8. Remove the plate from the freezer. Test the marmalade by placing a spoonful of it on the plate (see Sidebar, page 190). It should thicken promptly when you do so.

9. When the marmalade is finished, using potholders, pour the pot of marmalade into the smaller bowl. Scrape out every bit with the spatula. Set the bowl into the ice bath and stir the marmalade a few times to allow some of the heat to escape.

10. Cover the marmalade with plastic wrap so that the plastic is touching the surface of the marmalade, to keep a skin from forming. Once the marmalade is completely cooled, it can be stored in the refrigerator for up to 2 weeks.

Marmalade

Early in the year, our farmers' markets are overflowing with citrus: Valencia oranges, blood oranges (I always call these the fruit punch oranges, both for their color and flavor), Meyer lemons, Eureka lemons, Bearss limes, and tiny kumquats. Any combination of citrus fruits will work for marmalade; it depends only on your taste and what's available in your market.

Follow a general rule of equal parts chopped fruit and water. Boil that combination down by half, and add half as much sugar as there is fruit—for example, six cups of chopped fruit = six cups of water + three cups of sugar.

Rhubarb Hibiscus **Compote**

2 pounds rhubarb stalks
1¼ cups dark brown sugar
8 dried hibiscus flowers

I always know it's spring when I see the first stalks of rhubarb at the farmers' market. In this recipe, fresh rhubarb is cooked down into a bright-colored compote. Dried hibiscus flowers are traditionally used in *jamaica*, a Mexican agua fresca, and to make tea. You can find hibiscus flowers in tea shops and many grocery stores, especially Latin markets. Here, they brighten the pink hue of the rhubarb. This compote fills the corn-flour Rhubarb Tarts (see page 90) and also makes a delicious filling for fruit crisps and cobblers.

1. Rinse the rhubarb stalks and trim off the very ends. Unless the stalks are very slender, cut them in half lengthwise. Cut the rhubarb on the diagonal into ¾-inch chunks. You'll have about 6 cups of rhubarb; set aside 2 cups and put the remaining 4 cups into a medium heavy-bottomed pot (with about a 5-quart capacity).

2. Add the brown sugar and hibiscus flowers to the pot, give the mixture a few stirs, cover, and turn the heat to medium-low. (It's important to begin slowly so the rhubarb warms up and begins to release its liquid.) Cook the rhubarb mixture for about 15 minutes, covered, until the mixture is saucy.

3. Remove the cover and increase the heat to medium. Cook for 15 to 17 minutes, stirring continuously, until the rhubarb is completely broken down and thick enough that a spoon leaves a trail at the bottom of the pan.

4. Add the remaining rhubarb chunks to the pot and stir to combine.

5. Immediately pour the compote out onto a large plate or baking dish to cool. When the compote is cooled completely, remove the hibiscus flowers, squeezing any juice from them into the compote, and discard. The compote will keep in the refrigerator for up to 1 week.

Squash and **Apple** Compote

I love standing over the stove, cooking fruits and vegetables over high heat, listening to the hiss as they hit the pan, and watching their edges color. This is a slower process than you might think, as the ingredients need to sear and caramelize at just the right pace. It requires patience and practice to get it right. When finished, this compote is sweet and tender, brightened with a splash of apple cider vinegar. It's fantastic spooned over Quinoa Porridge (see page 138).

2 tablespoons unsalted
    butter
10 ounces butternut squash
    (about 2 cups), peeled
    and cut into $1/2$- to $3/4$-inch
    pieces
$1/4$ teaspoon kosher salt
1 pound tart apples
    (about 2 large apples),
    peeled and cut into
    $1/2$- to $3/4$-inch pieces
$1/4$ cup dark brown sugar
2 tablespoons apple cider
    vinegar

1. Melt the butter in a 12-inch sauté pan over a medium-high flame.

2. Add the squash and salt to the pan and toss to coat with the butter. Listen for the sizzle—this is a clue that your flame is hot enough—and adjust the heat as necessary. Cook the squash for 3 minutes without stirring or moving the pan; if the butter is browning, turn down the heat slightly.

3. Toss the squash and cook for 3 minutes more, again without stirring or moving the pan. The squash should be browning on the edges.

4. Add the apples and the sugar to the pan and toss to coat them in butter. Let the pan sit for 1 minute. Turn your flame down to medium-low and cook for about 10 minutes, until the apples and squash begin turning translucent and there is ample liquid in the pan. Increase the flame to medium and cook for about 20 minutes, tossing every 2 minutes, until the apples and squash are dark and caramelized and have absorbed all the syrup. If the pan becomes dry before the apples and squash are tender, add water 1 tablespoon at a time. This compote is best served hot from the pan.

Fig **Compote**

1/2 pound fresh figs

3 tablespoons unsalted
butter

3 tablespoons dark brown
sugar

3 tablespoons honey

Pinch of kosher salt

A good fig is sweet and juicy, reminiscent of caramel and red wine, with tiny seeds that pop when you bite into one. If you have the good fortune to have a farmers' market (or a neighbor's tree) nearby, use ripe fruit at the height of its season in late summer or early fall. Choose your favorite type of fig, or mix some varieties for additional flavor and color. Since ripe figs need very little cooking, I quickly toss them in a honey-butter syrup and then caramelize them under the broiler. This jammy compote was designed to be spooned over Barley Porridge (see page 71), but it's equally good atop pancakes, waffles, or even vanilla ice cream.

1. Preheat your broiler. Cut the stem off each fig, slice the fig in quarters, and set aside.
2. Add the butter, brown sugar, and honey to a cast-iron pan or a medium broilerproof sauté pan. Cook for about 1 minute over high heat, stirring frequently, until the syrup begins to bubble. Add the figs and stir to coat them with the syrup.
3. Place the pan under the broiler to caramelize the figs. Protecting your hand with an oven mitt or towel, swirl the pan a few times over the next 5 minutes to prevent the sugar and figs from burning. The figs are done when the syrup is thickened slightly and amber in color, and the edges of the figs are dark and glossy. Remove the pan from the broiler and serve the figs while they're still warm.

Pear Compote

This is a wonderful compote, made with pears sautéed in a maple-caramel sauce infused with cloves and vanilla bean. Choose pears that are ripe and flavorful, but not so ripe that they can't withstand a good sear in the pan. Spoon this compote over yogurt, fold it into Honeyed Crêpes (see page 139), or dollop some over Steel-Cut Oatmeal (see page 127).

2 medium pears, such as
   Anjou, ripe but firm
2 tablespoons unsalted
   butter
1/2 cup maple syrup
5 cloves
1/2 vanilla bean, split and
   scraped

1. Peel, halve, and core the pears. Slice the fruit into fat wedges, about 4 slices per half, and set aside.

2. Add the butter, maple syrup, and cloves to a 10-inch sauté pan. Add the vanilla bean pod and seeds to the pan. Cook over a medium flame, stirring frequently, until the butter is melted and the mixture begins to bubble. Increase the flame to medium-high and cook for about 1 minute, or until the caramel thickens slightly.

3. Carefully add the pears to the pan, placing them in an even layer. Listen for the sizzle—this is a clue that your flame is hot enough—and adjust the heat as necessary. Let the pears sear in the caramel, about 1 minute, without stirring them or moving the pan; if the fruit is moved around, it will not color.

4. Increase the flame to high and cook for about 8 minutes. The caramel will begin to bubble around the edges, moving toward the center as the juice reduces and the caramel darkens. If there are pockets of darker caramel, slide the pan gently back and forth to even out the sauce, being careful not to jostle the pears too much.

5. When the edges of the pears have darkened and the caramel is the color of molasses, flip the pears over with a metal offset spatula. Turn the flame off, leaving the pan on the stove until the caramel has stopped bubbling. Carefully fish the cloves and vanilla beans from the caramel with a fork. Serve the compote while still warm, as the caramel will harden slightly as it cools.

Apple **Butter**

4 pounds apples

1 orange

3 cinnamon sticks

6 whole allspice berries

6 whole cloves

3 cups apple juice

1/4 cup dark brown sugar

Flavor comes over time, whether you're talking about tree-ripened fruit or recipes that call for slow cooking. This rich apple butter is cooked for hours, as the apples darken and the sugars caramelize (don't worry—much of the cooking time is unattended). Eventually the apples become translucent, then turn auburn, then condense into a thick, jammy spread. Apple butter is delicious eaten straight from the pot, spooned onto crêpes, or spread onto bread for jam sandwiches. Pulling the cinnamon, cloves, and allspice from the pot after the first hour keeps their flavors subtly in the background.

1. Peel, quarter, and core the apples. Cut each quarter into thirds, then slice each third into pieces about as thick as your thumb.
2. Using a vegetable peeler, remove the peel from the orange in wide strips. Break the cinnamon sticks into smaller pieces. Gather the orange peel, cinnamon, allspice, and cloves into a circle of cheesecloth and tie it with a piece of kitchen twine. If you don't have cheesecloth, a scrap of porous white fabric will do.
3. Place the cut apples, spice bag, apple juice, and brown sugar in a 5- to 7-quart heavy-bottomed pot. Cover, place over high heat, and bring the mixture to a boil. Reduce the heat to medium-low and simmer, covered, for 2 hours.

4. After 1 hour, remove the spice bag, squeezing any juice from the bag back into the pot.
5. After 2 hours, some of the apple pieces should still be intact, while others will have broken down. The mixture will be fragrant, bubbling, and developing a rich color. Reduce the flame to low and cook, uncovered, for 1 1/2 hours more. During the last 30 minutes, stir the apple butter occasionally to prevent scorching. At the end of the cooking time, the apple butter should be thick and jammy, a dark reddish-brown in color, and deeply aromatic.
6. Depending on the apples you use, you may need to add water in the final hour of cooking. If the pot looks dry, add water 1/4 cup at a time, just enough to help break the apples down.
7. The apple butter may be slightly on the sweet side when eaten warm from the pot, but as it cools, its flavors come into their own. The apple butter will keep in the refrigerator for up to 2 weeks.

Note: Some tart apples that will work well in this recipe are Pink Lady, Braeburn, Anna, Ginger Gold, Gravenstein, and Granny Smith. Keep in mind that the quality of the apple you put in the pot will determine the quality of your finished product, so taste the apples that you plan on cooking with to make sure that their flavor and texture are what you want.

Fig Butter

In this recipe, dried figs are cooked in a syrup of sugar, red wine, port, and spices, and then puréed until very smooth. Adding butter at the end gives the jam a wonderful richness and a beautiful gloss. Once finished, the fig butter can be smeared over the dough in Figgy Buckwheat Scones (see page 80), creating a flavor-packed spiral. The scone recipe requires only half the amount of fig butter made here, so reserve the remaining spread for your morning toast—or use all the fig butter at once by doubling the scone recipe.

1/2 cup sugar

2 whole cloves

1 star anise

1 cup red wine

1/2 cup port

12 ounces dried Black Mission figs, stems removed

1/4 teaspoon cinnamon

4 ounces (1 stick) unsalted butter, softened

1. To poach the figs, measure 1/4 cup water and the sugar into a small heavy-bottomed saucepan. Stir the mixture together with a wooden spoon, incorporating the sugar without splashing it up the sides. If crystals do get on the sides of the pot, use a clean pastry brush dipped in water to wipe them off. (The goal is to prevent the syrup from crystallizing.) Add the cloves and star anise.

2. Bring the mixture to a boil over a medium flame and cook for 7 to 10 minutes, until the syrup is amber-colored. For even coloring, the flame should not come up around the outside of the pot.

3. Add the red wine, port, figs, and cinnamon, standing back a bit, as the syrup is hot. Don't panic when the syrup hardens; this is the normal reaction when liquids are added to hot sugar. Continue cooking the mixture over a medium flame for 2 minutes, until the sugar and wine blend.

4. Reduce the flame to low and simmer for 30 minutes, stirring occasionally. The figs will burble quietly as they are jostled together by the flame; they are ready when the wine has reduced by half. Remove the pan from the stove and cool to room temperature.

5. Fish out the star anise and cloves. Pour the cooled figs, with their liquid, into a food processor and purée until smooth, about 1 minute. Add the softened butter to the fig paste and process until smooth. The fig butter can be spread right onto the buckwheat scone dough or stored in the refrigerator for up to 1 month. If it is refrigerated, bring it to room temperature before using.

Sources

Flour

Kernels of grain are made up of bran, germ, and endosperm. In the milling of whole-grain flours, the entire kernel is ground. In the processing of flours not milled from whole grains, part or all of the bran and germ are removed, and much of the flavor and many of the nutrients are lost.

Some of you will be able to find whole-grain flours at your local market or natural-food store. Others will need to search the internet or place phone orders. This is a list of some of my favorite sources for whole-grain flours.

Anson Mills
1922-C Gervais Street
Columbia, SC 29201
(803) 467-4122
www.ansonmills.com

Arrowhead Mills
4600 Sleepytime Drive
Boulder, CO 80301
(866) 595-8917
www.arrowheadmills.com

Azure Standard
79709 Dufur Valley Road
Dufur, OR 97021
(541) 467-2230
www.azurestandard.com

Birkett Mills
163 Main Street
Penn Yan, NY 14527
(315) 536-3311
www. thebirkettmills.com

Bluebird Grains Farm
P. O. Box 1082
Winthrop, WA 98862
(509) 996-3526
www.bluebirdgrainfarms.com

Bob's Red Mill
Whole Grain Store and Visitors Center
5000 SE International Way
Milwaukie, OR 97222
(503) 607-6455
www.bobsredmill.com

Giusto's Vita-Grain
601 22nd Street
San Francisco, CA 94107
(866)972-6879
www.giustos.com

King Arthur
The Baker's Store
135 Route 5 South
Norwich, VT 05055
(800) 827-6836
www.kingarthurflour.com

Other Sources

BLiS Maple Syrup
3759 Broadmoor SE, Suite D
Grand Rapids, MI 49512
(616) 942-7545
www.blisgourmet.com/Products/syrupcart.html

24-cup aluminum 3.5 oz. muffin/cupcake pan
www.webstaurantstore.com
Smart & Final Stores in CA, AZ or NV

Valrhona Chocolate
www.wholefoods.com
www.chocolatesource.com
www.honestfoods.com

Stand Mixers
www.kitchenaid.com
(800)-541-6390

Oval Ice Cream Scoop
www.culinarycookware.com

Conversion Charts

Weight Equivalents

The metric weights given in this chart are not exact equivalents but have been rounded up or down slightly to make measuring easier.

AVOIRDUPOIS	METRIC
¼ oz	7 g
½ oz	15 g
1 oz	30 g
2 oz	60 g
3 oz	90 g
4 oz	115 g
5 oz	150 g
6 oz	175 g
7 oz	200 g
8 oz (½ lb)	225 g
9 oz	250 g
10 oz	300 g
11 oz	325 g
12 oz	350 g
13 oz	375 g
14 oz	400 g
15 oz	425 g
16 oz (1 lb)	450 g
1½ lb	750 g
2 lb	900 g
2¼ lb	1 kg
3 lb	1.4 kg
4 lb	1.8 kg

Volume Equivalents

These are not exact equivalents for American cups and spoons but have been rounded up or down slightly to make measuring easier.

AMERICAN	METRIC	IMPERIAL
¼ tsp	1.2 ml	
½ tsp	2.5 ml	
1 tsp	5.0 ml	
½ Tbsp (1.5 tsp)	7.5 ml	
1 Tbsp (3 tsp)	15 ml	
¼ cup (4 Tbsp)	60 ml	2 fl oz
⅓ cup (5 Tbsp)	75 ml	2.5 fl oz
½ cup (8 Tbsp)	125 ml	4 fl oz
⅔ cup (10 Tbsp)	150 ml	5 fl oz
¾ cup (12 Tbsp)	175 ml	6 fl oz
1 cup (16 Tbsp)	250 ml	8 fl oz
1¼ cups	300 ml	10 fl oz (½ pint)
1½ cups	350 ml	12 fl oz
2 cups (1 pint)	500 ml	16 fl oz
2½ cups	625 ml	20 fl oz (1 pint)
1 quart	1 liter	32 fl oz

Oven Temperature Equivalents

OVEN MARK	F	C	GAS
Very cool	250–275	130–140	½–1
Cool	300	150	2
Warm	325	170	3
Moderate	350	180	4
Moderately hot	375	190	5
	400	200	6
Hot	425	220	7
	450	230	8
Very hot	475	250	9

Acknowledgments

Writing this cookbook joined the two worlds that I feel the most comfortable in—cooking and family. There have been so many people that have encouraged and inspired me along the way.

First, I credit my agent, Betsy Amster, for seeing a book in me before I ever saw one in myself. Thank you for your guidance, keen eye, and the wealth of experience that you brought to this project. The best part is that we are neighbors; calling you at a moment's notice to ask you to pop over and taste my test recipes has definitely made this more fun.

To Luisa Weiss and everyone at Stewart, Tabori & Chang, for your belief and enthusiasm in this cookbook. Thank you, Luisa, for letting me be me; your editing has been spot on. I have so enjoyed the friendship that has begun and feel so lucky to have you as my guide.

To Quentin Bacon for your honest photography. Thank you for lending your talent to this book and capturing the hominess of my food. Thanks to Maeve Sheridan for sourcing our props. The photography weekend was truly magical.

To Elizabeth Norment for your detailed copy-editing. You over hauled this manuscript and organized it all with an eye for food. To Susi Oberhelman for your clear and concise design. The book is more beautiful than I could have imagined.

Amy Scattergood for your hard work: recipe testing, writing, and editing in a very short time. To Emily Green for shaping the proposal with me as well as your advice to write the recipes as though I've slid a tray of cookies in the oven, shut the door and turned around to tell a friend how they were made. Your advice was so liberating.

Marcella Capasso for your precision in testing the original proposal recipes.

Nancy Silverton, your palate and critical eye expanded and defined my world. Working with you taught me flavor, persistence, style, and belief in oneself. Thank you for taking me under your wing and for your warm introduction to this book.

To Sherry Yard at Spago and Christophe Moreau at Patina for the knowledge you instilled in me during my formative years in the kitchen. I am forever grateful. To Cecilia DeCastro for giving me the push to walk in the back door of Spago. Phyllis Vacharelli, your cooking school inspired me as a child and once I was ready to cook professionally.

To all of the chefs and cookbook authors who have inspired me, including: Claudia Fleming, Lindsey Shere, Deborah Madison, Patricia Wells, Rose Levy Beranbaum, Dorie Greenspan, Alice Medrich, Peter Reinhart, Margaret Fox, David Lebovitz, and Heidi Swanson.

My friends: Anna Delorefice, both in and out of the kitchen you are the best friend, baker, and sounding board there ever was. Your help was immeasurable during the writing of this book. Having you by my side always comforts me. Heather Ragsdale, for your sage advice throughout, always encouraging me to capture my voice—thank you, our friendship sustains me. Jessica Buonocore, our friendship began in the restaurant and continues in our kitchens. Thank you for reading the manuscript and for your critical notes, even while buried in the newness of Ate Café. Amelia Saltsman, you offered guidance from the very conception of this book and throughout, thank you. And to Roxana Jullapat

and Debra Matlock for even more recipe testing. Ellen Lawler, for your grandmother's Tzibeleh Kuchen recipe that inspired the (onionless!) Bird Crackers. Jodi Manby for proofreading. To Little Flower Candy Company for a table to write at and good food to eat.

To the farmers that grow the produce that inspires my cooking: John Hurley; Fitz Kelly; Mike Cirone; Bob Polito; Peter Schaner; Ken Lee; Harry's Berries; McGrath Farms; and Maryann, Paul, and Mark Carpenter.

Mom, you instilled in me your love of food, cooking, and entertaining through a childhood filled with homemade meals. Surely the freezer that was always stocked with oatmeal cookie dough inspired my career. It was you who taught me what it is to cook for your family.

Dad, thank you for standing by me even though you strongly disagreed with my decision to leave college and start cooking.

Thank you to the wonderful caregivers who took care of my girls while I was working: Cristina, Sarah, Nancy, and the teachers at nursery school.

For my love, Thomas, our world has grown so much since those long-ago days on the line cooking together. Thank you for your critical palate and honest interest in this project. Your support is so very important to me.

To my two little girls, Lola and Sofia, for eagerly eating most everything your mama makes. You two inspire me to create the food that we eat.

Index

Page references in *italic* refer to illustrations.

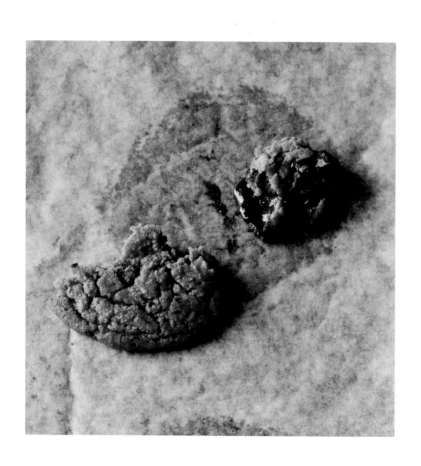

8|14-21

8|14-21

2|16-22